Pre-Exilic Prophecy

Words of Warning,
Dreams of Hopes,
Spirituality of Pre-Exilic Prophets

by

Richard J. Sklba

A Michael Glazier Book
THE LITURGICAL PRESS
Collegeville, Minnesota

About the Author

Bishop Richard J. Sklba studied theology at the Gregorian University (S.T.L.) and at the Angelicum (S.T.D.). He received his S.S.L. from the Pontifical Biblical Institute and studied Modern Hebrew at Ulpan Etzion in Jerusalem. He has taught in Rome and in America and was consecrated auxiliary bishop of Milwaukee in 1979.

A Michael Glazier Book
published by
THE LITURGICAL PRESS

1   2   3   4   5   6   7   8   9

Library of Congress Cataloging-in-Publication Data
Sklba, Richard J.
   Pre-exilic prophecy : words of warning, dreams of hope,
spirituality of pre-exilic prophets / by Richard J. Sklba.
      p.   cm. — (Message of biblical spirituality ; v. 3)
"A Michael Glazier book."
Includes bibliographical references and indexes.
ISBN 0-8146-5569-6 (pbk.)
   1. Bible. O.T. Prophects (Nevi 'im)—Criticism, interpretation,
etc. 2. Spiritual life—Biblical teaching. 3. Jews—History—To
586 B.C. 4. Prophets. I. Title. II. Series.
BS1505.6.S7 1990
224—dc20   90-62043
                                                  CIP

Contents

Preface and Introduction

In the Prologue of Saint Jerome's famous *Commentary on Isaiah*, he writes, "The person who does not know Scripture, does not know the power and wisdom of God". This surely presumes the biblical understanding of "know," namely thoughtful and caring perusal in faith, and concern for all the poetic human nuances of language as well as for accurate intellectual information. Such is *Lectio Divino* which is the scope of this series. It is a perilous venture to indulge in such a task for others, for in the last analysis God's Spirit operates in each person richly and uniquely. Such is the mystery and challenge of spirituality which is also the scope of this series.

In the comments which follow, I presume the contribution of historical literary criticism and proceed in a spirit of "post-critical spirituality" to reflect on the Sacred Text and the times to which the Prophetic Spirit spoke. This volume is limited to a consideration of the pre-exilic prophets. For an excellent presentation of the spirituality of those prophets following the destruction of Jerusalem and the Babylonian Exile, the reader is encouraged to consult the companion work by Dr. Eileen Schuller, OSU.

I ask the readers to use this volume with the Bible in hand as well, checking every scriptural citation and lingering over the text in order to enter into dialogue with each prophet and the God they served. Their struggle with the Will of the Lord, and the transformation they experienced in the process, represents their spirituality. Studying their words has made them my friends. I can only pray that each reader will develop a similar bond of respect and affection for these marvelous men and women. They are heroes of faith for all times. The questions at the end of each chapter are intended to extend the prophetic message into our modern age.

Except for a few instances I have refrained from references to the New Testament in order to allow these pre-exilic prophets to speak on their own. The richness of their message should not be short-circuited by too rapid a leap into the Christian context.

In speaking of their God, I have chosen to use Lord as a respectful term consonant with the Hebrew tradition except when I deliberately desired to accent the unique nature of the God of the Covenant; then the name of Yahweh was invoked.

In almost all instances I have cited the New American Bible, departing from that practice only when the flavor of the text seemed to suggest another rendition which remains my own.

I take the occasion to thank former students and friends whose intellectual curiosity and faith enabled me to grow in respect for the Hebrew prophets over the years. I take responsibility for the limitations of this volume and bless the Lord of the Universe for the fact that they are not more numerous. In particular, I wish to express appreciation to Dr. Carolyn Osiek, RSCJ, the editor of the series for her patience and encouragement, and Sister Rose Stinefast, SSND, who provided invaluable assistance as I used the project to enter the world of word processors. Prophets always seem to push their audience into new and unexpected realms of God's creation!

Richard J. Sklba

The Feast of Saint Jerome

Dedicated To Archbishop Jean Jadot
Apostolic Delegate In The United States
1973-1980
A Man Of God's Spirit
And Servant Of The Church

1

Mysterious Beginnings

The power and the presence of God confronts us often in life, sometimes challenging us with frightening alternatives, at other times strengthening and supporting decisions which we have taken. The mystery of God is as pervasive as the air we breathe or the elements of the world within which we move. God may address us through the hostile voice of an antagonist, the probing inquiry of a friend or the whining plea of a stranger in need. The circumstances of each phase of our lives demand responses daily. The opportunities for generosity and the occasions for asserting our integrity are all related to the way God encourages us to grow. To live is to grow, to change and to respond in fresh ways. Our God is a living God with whom we walk and by whose Spirit-breath we live.

Often classical prophets like Amos, Hosea, or Jeremiah are proposed to us as models of spirituality. We remember them as outstanding figures who took God seriously, even at the cost of friends or life itself. They are sometimes presented as rebellious solitary figures who struck out against injustice and institutions. Indeed sometimes they did, but always as a result of their own conviction and within the context of their communities of faith.

To portray them as romantic individuals forever poised in controversy, arrogantly rejecting all forms of ritual worship, or busily predicting the future is to cling to stereotypes quite distant from the facts of the matter. They said what had to be said because they spoke for God. They demanded truly transforming and challenging worship because they understood that God was satisfied with nothing less.

The truth of the matter is that the prophets of Israel did not predict the future because they were too busy giving expression to the present. Like poets of all ages, they saw reality at its deepest level. They took a long loving look at that reality and either saw God or the absence of God. From that divine epicenter moved waves of tenderness or anger as yet unexperienced by the merchants and farmers of Israel or Judah. Prophets knew the vitality of God and spoke accordingly. They sensed the first stirrings of divine action. Only to that extent did they paint the future.

What does it mean to be prophetic? When do we label our own actions or opinions with that term? The newspapers use the word regularly, but the dictionary is woefully unhelpful. If we would use the word in its true sense, we would be required to find something which goes against the grain of common opinion, either because the stand upholds gentleness when most others are angry, or because it assumes the tone of ringing denunciation when no one else can see what all the fuss is about. Find something that's right, but perhaps not popular. Find something rooted in the mystery of God, or expressing a true facet of God's will for the world and those who live within it. That's prophetic!

A parade of individuals cross before our mind's eye when we speak of the early prophets of Israel. They were men and women sought out for advice and counsel, individuals who stood up to the king and his court, or who denounced the priest and his sanctuary attendants. They were women and men who offered consolation and comfort to ordinary folks. Some of these prophets are known by name. Their words have been gathered and preserved. Very human struggles of doubt and uncertainty (Jeremiah), love and rejection (Hosea), trust and confidence (Isaiah), or righteous anger on behalf of the shabbily treated poor (Amos and Micah) indicate the areas of life within which these prophets met their God. Precisely in those arenas of life they struggled with the divine will and wearily announced the results of each round.[1]

While most of the familiar prophets of Israel were in fact men, a closer inspection of the Biblical witness reveals the significant presence of women as well. The song of victory at the Reed Sea was attributed to Miriam (Ex 15:20), and this was a major event in the history of God's people. Although her portrait seems quite different from the profiles of other major prophetic figures recounted in Scripture, Miriam was designated as a "prophetess" and exercised some leadership at the major foundational event of Israel as well as in the wilderness community. The fact that she has received this title cautions us lest we have too narrow a notion of the function of prophet in Israel.[2]

---

[1] A complete bibliographical listing of additional references for further reading is impossible. For a general introduction in historical context and sequence, see B. Anderson. *Understanding the Old Testament,* 4th edition (Prentice-Hall, 1986). Another contemporary work with excellent references is J. Blenkinsopp, *A History of Prophecy in Israel* (Westminster, 1982). See also the more extensive suggestions for further reading at the end of this volume.

[2] For a fascinating study on Miriam, see R. Burns, *Has the Lord indeed Spoken Only Through Moses?,* SBL Dissertaion Series 84 (Scholars Press, 1987).

Likewise, the prophetess Huldah is remembered for her role in interpreting the scroll found in the temple during the liturgical renovations under king Josiah in the seventh century B.C.E. Her insightful recognition of the text as an authentic covenant with imminent punishment for years of neglect and disobedience (2 K 22:14-20) led to the adoption of the law, probably some early form of the Deuteronomic corpus, as the law of the land. Her action, endorsed by Josiah, changed the tradition of Israel from a religion of the Covenant to one of the Book. Huldah made a major contribution indeed! Similarly, Deborah was recalled as a great prophetess/warrior (Jgs 4:4). These figures should be kept in mind during the following pages and comments. The patriarchal structure may have been more common, but women played significant roles in the history and spirituality of Israelite and Judean prophecy.

Early Prophetic Groups

"As you enter that city, you will meet a band of prophets in prophetic state; coming down from the high place, preceded by lyres, tambourines, flutes and harps." (1 Sam 10:5)

There were others, however, as we page through the texts of Scripture, people known only because they belonged to a group bearing the name "sons of the prophets." These anonymous individuals were attached to a central leader. They gathered at shrines or highplaces on occasion and then moved across the countryside. When young Saul encountered them, they were carrying kids or goats (probably for sacred sacrificial meals) and with the aid of tambourines and dance fell into ecstatic states. The text cited above represents a command given by the prophet Samuel to young Saul. The prophet promised that Saul would encounter an ecstatic group whose spirit would embrace him as well, with the result that he would also become ecstatic, and indeed "be changed into another man" (10:6)! For Saul the ecstasy was not only contagious, it was also viewed as an authenticating sign of his own vocation and mission as future king.

These roving bands are the earliest form of prophecy encountered in Hebrew Scripture. Miriam, the sister of Moses, was designated a prophetess (Ex 15:20). Genealogy was used in Israel and neighboring cultures to express association and some commonality in life. Thus, that Miriam should be remembered as a sister to Aaron and Moses in the Levitical genealogies (Nm 26:29 and 1 Chr 5:29) suggests a partnership of deep and lasting significance. She also was with a band who celebrated in song and dance the victory of Yahweh over the Pharaoh's armies. Always in some form of community, these prophets underscore the social aspect of all religion in the ancient world.

Modern individualism does not possess the same instinct. In fact, recent attempts at liturgical renewal have been forced to enter a long struggle to reestablish the communal dimension of prayer and authentic religious experience. It is a people whom Yahweh chose for his own (Ex 19:3-8), and individuals were included only to the degree that they shared that bond.

From the very beginning of prophecy in Israel these groups were closely related to "priestly" activities. They gathered at the highplaces for sacrifice and sacred feasting. Like Samuel reproving Saul, they declared sacrifice acceptable to God or rejected it, because they knew what was truly pleasing to God (1 Sam 9:27-10:1). They used symbolic actions at times to illustrate their messages or revelation, and thus to give graphic force to the power of their words. Ritual and worship was the arena of early priest and prophet alike.

In later centuries the two roles of priest and prophet became more sharply differentiated in Israel. The priest tended to emphasize the history of Yahweh's actions in behalf of his people and concluded the credal recitation of salvific history with an affirmation that God was present. Even the Christian Eucharist follows the same general line of inner structure. The prophet however began with the emphatic conviction of divine presence and concluded to certain inevitable forms of action which God would surely take in view of the situation. Such methods of interpreting God's spirit only developed over long ages, based on ancient traditions. Gradually, separate forms of communication for priest or prophet evolved which were only vaguely present from the beginning.

Even after the figures of priest and prophet became distinct roles in Israel, the function of prophet was a regular part of community worship. Prophets were readily available at shrine or temple to give oracles of salvation in response to prayers and petitions. They gave oracles to the king in moments of decision, sometimes speaking what they knew the king wanted to hear (2 Chr 18:5-34). In those instances the prophets demonstrated the hazard of being too close to the institution, thus becoming blind to the true will of the Lord whom they claimed to serve. At times these 'cult prophets" were unable to see the absence of the deeper level of religiosity demanded by a person like Jeremiah. Anyone whose salary and sustenance is provided by the temple needs to be vigorously vigilant lest in place of serving the Lord, they merely enhance the human institution. Successive centuries don't remove the challenge or the temptation.

Similarly, the distinction between prophet and community

leader (judge/king) is a later clarification. Deborah was prophetess and judge (Jgs 4:4). Samuel was judge (1 Sam 7:15) and prophet (9:9). Saul was king (10:1.24) and associated with prophetic groups at times (19:23-24). In that age as in ours, spirit-given charisms were gradually given stable and predictable forms. They were clarified by the experiences of life and enriched each other.

Visions

"Who has stood in the council of the Lord, to see him and to hear his word?" (Jer 23:18)

In those early years prophetic bands often experienced the powerful presence of Yahweh as an all-absorbing reality. Ecstatic consciousness of the divine led them to associate many different human experiences with the immediate presence of God. The early title for prophets was *ro'eh*, "the seeing one" (1 Sam 9:9), for the holy person of God was able to perceive the mind of God as well as the true state of things in God's world. The prophet Balaam described himself as the one "whose eyes were open" (Nm 24:3.15). Samuel saw that Saul's lost asses were found (1 Sam 10:16) and Micaiah ben Imlah saw Israel scattered in battle like sheep without a shepherd (1 K 22:18f).

Visions continued with later classical prophets as well. The very title of the book of Amos describes the entire book as a vision (Am 1:1). The introduction which refers to "the words which Amos saw" makes sense only when we remember that the Hebrew term *dabar* "word" means event as well as spoken phrase. Toward the end of the book, Amos includes a series of visions related to the destruction of the northern kingdom of Israel and the ruin of the temple: grasshoppers devouring the crops (7:1-3), a raging and consuming fire from the depths of the earth (vv. 4-6), a measuring plumbline (vv. 7-9), harvested summer fruit foreshadowing the end of growth (8:1-3), and finally in a vision of terror, Yahweh smashing the temple doorways and killing the fleeing worshipers (9:1)! Isaiah saw the awesome presence of Yahweh with robes cascading in incense down into the temple (Is 6:1-3).

Jeremiah saw blossoming almond trees (called "watching" trees in the parlance of his day since they were quick to note the coming of Spring) and a boiling kettle whose froth was blown from the north (Jer 1:11-15). In Jeremiah's later bitter disputes with those prophets whom he denounced as false, he dismissed them as speaking a vision of their own fancy (23:16), not from authentic experiences in the Council of the Lord. In the text cited above, Jeremiah has some harsh things to say about the immorality of some of the professional prophets of Jerusalem (23:14). He laments about the ease with which they promise "peace" to their followers (v. 17), and contends in the name of the Lord, "I did not send these prophets, yet they ran; I did not speak to them, yet they prophesied" (v. 21). Had his opponents really stood in the Council room of God they would have preached other messages, and therefore, Jeremiah rejected them out of hand. The vision was the final mark of authenticity for Jeremiah!

In eerie surrealistic fashion Ezekiel described the God of judgment (Ez 1:4-28) and recounted the glory of Yahweh leaving the temple in disgust (Ez 10:23). Each vision produced new insight. Later apocalypticists became increasingly detailed as their elaborate visions described the mysterious reality about to break forth into the plain sight of everyone. Today as always, those who would be prophetic require more than 20/20 vision. To possess such keen sharpened spiritual insight is essential to the prophetic task. The Lord's question to Amos (7:8; 8:2) or Jeremiah (1:11.13), namely "what do you see?" is in fact addressed to everyone!

The question of vision, however, poses one of the more troubling issues for prophecy, whether in the age of Israel or in our own. How is anyone to judge whether a self-proclaimed prophet has truly encountered God? How is one to know if the mandate is worthy of obedience? Not everyone who comes running over the hill, claiming to speak in the name of God, merits a hearing. The book of Deuteronomy represents a tradition which attempted to take prophecy seriously. Consequently, several criteria were proposed for the discerning community.

In some instances, the community was instructed to ask if the prophet or dreamer was leading toward God or astray from the way directed by the Lord (Dt 13:2-6). The response was simple enough and the measuring stick obvious, but what about those genuine prophets who lead people away from popular but inadequate conceptions of God towards a more profound insight? The new was not always wrong. Only after further reflection by the community could a more correct judgment be made. How was one to tell?

Another criterion developed by Deuteronomy suggested that the community should simply "wait and see" if the oracle was fulfilled or verified (18:21-22). But a community couldn't wait forever, at least not one which was serious about the Will of God in urgent and significant matters!

In the final analysis, the only measurement for judging the visions of others was that of prayer. The open heart of the community and its leader to the presence of the Lord enabled

others to see if the new vision was somehow consistent with
their experience of Yahweh over the years. The deeper meaning
of their stories of faith had its own pattern and spiritual logic.
New visions and mandates which presumed the same values
and used the same values and the same images were probably
more authentic. The radically conservative prophet had the
greater chance of being the bearer of an authentic vision. The
community in prayer was able to know the difference.
Meanwhile, communities received the leaders and prophets
they deserved. Those truly open and humble before the Lord
eventually came to know God's will. Visions were tested
against the spiritual sensitivity of the community. It always
remained a risky business however, and Israel could never be
absolutely sure. "Walking humbly before the Lord" (Mic 6:8)
represents the best advice for avoiding a self-righteous presumption that we already know all there is to know about the
Will of the Lord for us!

Origins Of Ecstatic Groups

"When they were going from there to Gibeah, a band of
prophets met Saul and the spirit of God rushed upon him, so
that he joined them in their prophetic state." (1 Sam 10:10).

Paging through the records of Israel's faith, we notice that
Israel's first encounters with the roving bands of ecstatics
occurred only after entering Canaan. Some would say that this
type of ecstatic religious experience represented an expression
of the fertility cults germane to the people living in the land
into which Israel came. This group of scholars would say that
it remained a temptation for centuries, encouraged by

neighboring nations and subsequent rulers eager to court the political alliances and the wealth of others.

In the minds of such scholars, the group encountered by Saul would have been associated with the fertility cults practiced on the high places of Canaan. Saul would have shared their "spirit", not only their enthusiastic and orgiastic ritual, but also their values and character. Such would be the presumption among those who saw the ecstatic prophets as native to the territory into which Moses and Joshua led the Hebrew people.

Other scholars see the ecstatic experience of religion as reflective of a certain type of personality, less coldly rationalistic and more inclined to the emotional facets of human experience.[3] I agree. Such temperaments can be found in all ages and parts of the earth. While some cultures and religious traditions may tend to repress or prohibit emotional expression in the context of legitimate worship, others instead celebrate its presence as divine gift, or at least they provide acceptable forms for incorporating emotions into community life and worship.

The general Canaanite culture seems to be an example of the latter. So was Israel. Emotion was a welcome element in worship and the expression of faith. Those freed from Egypt welcomed the roving prophets because for both parties religious experience was of its nature communal and covenantal, wholistic and embracing the entire human person. Prophets "on the move" reminded Israel of earlier experiences in the wilderness. Representatives of these wandering groups of more strict observance remained present in Judah even down to the time of Jeremiah when the Rechabites were viewed as similar to the Amish of our day. According to a conversation recorded

---

[3] J. Lindblom, *Prophecy in Ancient Israel* (Fortress, 1967).

during the final days of Jerusalem before the destruction of the
city by the Babylonians, the Rechabites proudly stated that
they refused to drink wine, build houses, or sow fields, but
insisted on living in tents like their ancestors (Jer 35:6-10).
The roving bands of earlier days as well as subsequent centuries
showed the openness of Israel to such ecstatic movements.
They were more than curiosities which came with the culture
of the new land.

The same impulse which led Saul to recognize Samuel as
authentic in the worship of the highplace (1 Sam 10), namely
the expression of prophetic prayer by rhythm and dance, leads
contemporary Jewish Hasidic communities to pray with
rhythmic bodily movement and to incorporate every sense
into their modern synagogue worship. Here again, within the
context of each distinct cultural heritage, the tradition of the
prophets can make a contribution to modern life and faith.

Unrestrained enthusiasm, without the benefit of ritual
form and tested tradition, can be perilous. The history of
religious experience is fraught with examples of communities
virtually shipwrecked by such practices and the aberrations
they inspired. Nevertheless, the biblical witness regarding the
origins of the prophetic movement remains a healthy reminder
of the necessary role of all facets of human nature in community response to the God of revelation and life.

The Hebrew word most commonly used for prophet in
Israel, namely, *nabi'*, serves to illustrate the ambiguity of the
origins of this institution in Israel. As the editorial note
inserted into the story of Saul and Samuel indicated, the
person formerly called a Seer later became a prophet/*nabi'*
(1Sam 9:9). Philologically the word has been highly controverted among students of ancient Near Eastern Semitic and
cognate languages. Some saw a reference to "bubbling up,

frothing over, being mad or ecstatic." Others saw a relationship to the Akkadian verb to "call, be sent, announce." The very history of the word may illustrate the complex history of the institution in Israel.

All early forms of prophetic activity found expression in some type of communal experience. This reality never disappeared. Although no reference is made to the followers or associates of Balaam (Nm 22-24), subsequent figures are almost invariably presented with other persons closely involved in the prophet's activity and vision. Just as the sons of the priest Eli were associated with the worship at Shiloh (1 Sam 1:3), so also the sons of the prophet Samuel were associated with him at the highplace of Ramah (7:17-8:3). It seems wise to note that such references do not automatically refer to their physical children, but rather can be presumed to suggest association with the work at hand, just as modern trade unions might refer to members as "sister" or "brother." Unfortunately, as the text indicates, each group linked to Eli or Samuel was subsequently rejected as blatantly self-serving and greedily disobedient before Yahweh. This violation of faith opened the way for Saul who stood in line for leadership when the associations around Eli or Samuel were rejected as legitimate successors. Saul encountered Samuel at the highplace with some thirty others (9:22). Saul also met bands of prophets, falling into ecstasy with song and music, at various turning points in his life. Prophetic groups were present at the affirmation of his election (10:5.10f) and when he attempted to kill David (19:19-24).

Elijah associated Elisha with his work (1 K 19:19-21), as did Elisha in choosing Gehazi as his servant in turn (2 K 4:12). Neither pursued a ministry in total isolation. Bands of prophets connected with the shrines at Bethel and Jericho roamed along the Jordan. They are mentioned repeatedly in the wondrous account of Elijah's final disappearance in the fiery chariot (2 K 2:3.5.15). Isaiah's own wife was called a prophetess (Is 8:3), leading a whimsical reader to speculate about the possibility of some early form of "team ministry" between the spouses. Isaiah was also commanded to give testimony to his disciples (v. 16). Jeremiah shared his mission with Baruch who recorded the prophet's words and even spoke them in the temple when Jeremiah was unable to do so in person (Jer 36:4-8). Even Ezekiel found himself the center of popular attention from crowds who saw him as a "ballad singer with a pleasant voice and a clever touch" (Ez 33:32). After the Exile and after the rebuilding of the temple, even choirs were called prophets (1 Chr 25:1, 23). Thus the social nature of Israel's prophecy continued into the psalms! All the way through, the social context of prophetic gifts remained a constant. The completely solitary prophet is no prophet at all. A similar gift today requires a similarly supportive and challenging community.

Many religious today would find in the first organizational years and the foundational experiences of their vowed religious communities in the Church, a pattern similar to that of the early prophetic movements in Israel. A keen sense of the divine will, aimed at a specific task not seen by contemporaries, attracting a small group of similar minded "visionaries." Doesn't this sound like the charism of a religious community? How about the founders and foundresses of parishes in early American settlements?

The Prophet's Call

"To whomever I send you, you shall go; whatever I command you, you shall speak" (Jer 1:7).

In the midst of the people and often associated with others, the prophet was distinguished as one who experienced Yahweh's power in a profound and sometimes shattering manner. Common everyday experiences became striking reflections and signs of the deeper reality of Yahweh's plans. The flowering almond (Jeremiah) and the smoke-filled temple (Isaiah) were occasions for an overwhelming insight into the activity of Yahweh which was about to burst into full view.

Those divine plans were at times unexpected and unwelcome to the people of Judah or Israel whose leaders had been repeating a totally different message. Isaiah, for example, promised divine potection for Zion and begged for total trust in Yahweh's power, while the king insisted on busying himself with military alliances and strategic defense of the royal citadel. Although the prophet insisted on confidence in God alone, the king was totally preoccupied with repairing the ramparts and preparing adequate cisterns for siege (Is 7:3-9).

A century later Jeremiah announced the destruction of the temple (Jer 7:13-15) and a long exile for leaders and sacred temple instruments captured by the Babylonians in 597 B.C.E. In response, mischievous children in the streets mocked him with the title "Terror all around" (20:10). Jeremiah responded by giving the same name "Terror on every side" to the very popular priest at the Temple, Pashhur, who punished the prophet by scourging him and placing him in the stocks overnight (vv. 2-3). Those dedicated to good order, even during the liturgical renewal under king Josiah, were not pleased by the prophet's message. Later Jeremiah continued to repeat the speech even though Hananiah, a very popular prophet about town, was eloquent in promising a speedy demise for Babylon and a prompt return of captives and temple objects (28:1-17).

Precisely because of the prophet's personal experience of God, he or she realized that the divine will was at variance from the common expectations of the age, even of the respected religious leaders of the day. Therefore prophets felt compelled to speak the truth of the matter. Amos reflected his inner sense of personal urgency when he described the dynamic of prophetic consciousness by stating, "The lion roars, who will not be afraid; the Lord God speaks, who will not prophesy!" (Am 3:8). Jeremiah attempted to suppress his inner convictions without success, "I said to myself, I will not mention him, I will speak in his name no more. But then it became like fire burning in my heart, imprisoned in my bones; I grow weary holding it in, I cannot endure it" (Jer 20:9).

The call of Jeremiah represents a perfect example of the beginning of a prophetic vocation. A careful reading of the first chapter as presently found in the book of Jeremiah will illustrate our reflections (1:4-19). Perhaps the chapter was a final composition, added to the oracles of Jeremiah at the end of his life or even after his death. Only then were things perfectly clear. In the thirteenth year of Josiah (v. 2) Jeremiah would probably have been a young man in his later teens. Living with a sense of inner destiny, he still shied away from any call to prophetic leadership or public denunciation, claiming his inability to speak (v. 6) due to age. The literal sense of the verse is that Jeremiah was still a *na'ar*, a minor without full recognition in the community. The objection of Jeremiah reminds us of a similar hesitancy on the part of Moses (Ex 4:10) and both illustrate what God can do with human partners, however limited and weak!

The response of God to Jeremiah's qualms almost borders on a rebuke, as cited above (v. 7). The ability and the authority are given by the Lord in the very act of conferring a mission.

Fear is forbidden "because I am with you to deliver you, says the Lord" (vv. 8.19). Jeremiah even experienced something akin to the Lord touching his lips and placing divine words in the human prophet's mouth (v. 9). The visions of the almond watching tree (v. 11) and the boiling caldron blown upon from the north (v. 13) may have occurred later in the prophet's life and been placed in this context by a subsequent editor. Likewise the reference to the hostile nations sitting in victorious judgment at the gates of a destroyed Jerusalem may be a later clarification. Life is always understood backwards, but lived forwards. The call of Jeremiah was no exception. He perceived a mission received from the Lord, and a strong command to be on with it in spite of his inner doubts and fears. The Lord who sent him could transform him.

The call of Jeremiah was not totally negative. While his vision did eventually focus upon the imminent arrival of the powerful Babylonian armies and the destruction of the Temple which had guaranteed God's presence in the midst of the nation, Jeremiah saw his task as one called "to build and to plant" as well as "to root up and to tear down" (v. 10). He envisioned the return of the northern nations which had been exiled after the Assyrian victory over the city of Samaria in 722/721 B.C.E. To that end he advised Rachel, symbol of the Northern Israelite mother mourning the absence of her exiled children, to dry her tears since they would return home again by the power of the Lord (31:15-17)! With utter confidence Jeremiah could announce such remarkably joyful news with the formal introductory words, "Thus says the Lord" (vv. 7.15.16).

Considerable scholarly work has been invested in exploring the origins of this familiar prophetic phrase, "Thus says the Lord." Those who prefaced their utterances with that formula seemed to act as messengers from the divine council. They came with words of judgment or special oracles in the name of God. In an age of oral communication the technical form was immediately recognized by everyone. It seems to have been used regularly by messengers from the royal court or from dignitaries of a neighboring town. The formula laid claim to authority.[4]

Personal experience, inner evaluation and sorting out (almost like the action of the fireplace grating which shakes off the ashes to reveal the burning coals of Yahweh's purpose in the world), and communication represent the three basic elelments of the prophetic call. Because these same elements also reveal the inner dynamic of our struggle with God's Spirit, they illustrate prophetic spirituality and provide insight into our own lives as well. Today women and men alike find these elements in common with the prophets of old.

Another way of viewing the prophets of Israel has recently offered us an intriguing and captivating prism. In each case the prophets remembered by name provided an imaginative alternative to the social and religious reality experienced by their age. Just as Moses led the people of Egypt toward a fresh and new vision of freedom in contrast to the royal domination of the Pharaoh, so each major prophet was inspired with an alternative for God's people. Elijah was able to imagine a nation completely loyal and dedicated to Yahweh alone. Amos imagined a society built upon full and final justice for all rather than the exploitation which he witnessed everywhere. Isaiah dreamed of such trust and confidence that little children would even play unharmed at the adder's den, and lambs

---

[4]C. Westermann, *Basic Forms of Prophetic Speech* (Westminister, 1967).

could lie down with lions. Each prophet found people to share a dream proposed by a God powerful enough to bring that dream into reality. The prophets of Israel are men and women with truly creative imagination.[5]

Royal Contemporaries

"Ahab came to meet Elijah, and when he saw Elijah, said to him, 'Is it you, you disturber of Israel?' 'It is not I who disturb Israel, he answered, 'but you and your family, by forsaking the commands of the Lord and following the Baals'" (1 K18:16-18).

Sometimes prophets were called upon to confront the king in his error. Prophets pointed out to the king any sinful violation of the Lord's commandments or royal departure from decent covenantal behavior. When David had Uriah killed so ignominiously after the king's adultery with Bathsheba, the prophet Nathan came forward with the parable of the poor man's lamb (2 Sam 12:1-12). It evoked a terrible judgment of self-condemnation from the lips of David himself. Unfortunately, not every prophet was able to achieve such instantaneous success.

Similarly, when Ahab had profited from the shameful murder of poor Naboth, Elijah sought out the king and confronted him face to face for his crime. It was not Elijah who was guilty of disturbing the status quo in Israel, but rather Ahab himself with his royal disregard for the human rights and convenantal obligations rightfully due his subjects (1 K 18:16-18). Once again a prophet stood his ground before the king.

[5] W. Brueggemann, *The Prophetic Imagination* (Fortress, 1978).

One of the many curiosities of Hebrew history stems from the fact that, for the most part, prophets emerged as individual persons with concrete name and history only during the age of the kings of Judah and Israel. When the royal house of Israel disappeared on the occasion of the victory of Assyria in 722 B.C.E., prophets were no longer mentioned among the peoples of the north. Similarly, when the Davidic dynasty mysteriously evaporated after the return of the exiles to Jerusalem in 538 B.C.E., so did individual prophetic figures. Only A few like Haggai and Zephaniah encouraged the rebuilding of the temple. The age of post-exilic prophecy is often dismissed as theologically thin and preoccupied with cultic ritual. The companion volume in this exploration into prophetic spirituality will show the fallacy of such a view.[6] Ezekiel had begun his prophetic work at the time of the Exile and the humble figure known simply as Deutero-Isaiah had made an enormous contribution, but individual prophets of magnitude were no longer recognized by name. They were somehow absorbed into the text. Anonymous figures added later portions to existing prophetic books, but the age of the prophets in Israel was somehow drawn to a conclusion. A new era for prophecy had dawned; the earlier age was over. At the time of the Chronicles, choir members alone were called prophets. This is a very curious fact of history.

Perhaps the concrete individuality of the royal leader (usually designated and anointed by Yahweh through prophetic intervention) required a constant critique to assure that he remained faithful to Yahweh. The prophet served as a partner in dialogue, although sometimes very acrimoniously,

---

[6]For a rich treatment, see the companion volume to this study in the same series, namely that of E. Schuller, *Post-Exilic Prophecy* (Glazier, 1987).

throughout his reign. When the king was no longer present on the scene, the prophet's task was less urgent.

Perhaps king and royal chapel were so closely aligned during that period that an independent prophetic voice was needed to keep both honest before the mystery of Israel's God. When the alliance was dissolved, the prophet's task was less urgent.

Perhaps the classical prophet was first remembered by name because he in turn was the first to pronounce divine judgment upon the person of the king by name. When the king no longer functioned as such, the prophetic messenger from the heavenly council was no longer needed for that task.

Perhaps the transformation of oral revelation into written canonical form (during the exile or shortly thereafter) provided a more stable expression of Yahweh's will. Since the demise of classical prophecy roughly coincided with the rise of written Scriptures, this may be yet another possible explanation for the disappearance of prophets from Judah.

Perhaps the task of discerning true from false prophecy, in spite of the various criteria developed by Israel over the years (Dt 13:2-6; 18:21f; Jer 28:8f), finally proved too difficult and uncertain for Israel. In that age as well as in our own, so many prophets came proclaiming contradictory messages, each claiming to speak in the name of God. Perhaps a more definitive point of reference was necessary for stability.

There are, therefore, many explanations for the fact that classical prophecy existed for only those centuries which roughly coincided with the existence of the monarchy, and then faded from the scene as a vital and significant force in the history of Israel. Who are the prophets of any age? Do they tend to achieve preeminence and publicity in times of political oppression and authoritarian rule? Does the existence and powerful voice of Oscar Romero or Helder Camara in the South American experience of oppression of the poor provide a scenario capable of explaining the rise and demise of prophecy in Israel? Does the existence of ruthless government forces provide the needed foil for the rise of prophets? Or, is it rather the case that prophets cease to speak when absolutely no one listens?

Some prophets supported the king and his policies. Hananiah was sure that the king was correct in expecting the prompt return of sacred vessels from Babylon, and that Jeremiah was wrong. The text makes the ironical note that Hananiah was from Gibeon (Jer 28:1), a people long remembered in Scripture for their deceitfulness (Jos 9:3-6). In the longer view of history, Hananiah is only remembered because he had the haphazard misfortune of opposing the one whose vision was proven correct. Those who spoke against the grain, those who resisted the flow of royal decree when history demonstrated its inner error, were the ones whose memory was treasured, at least by later generations. The innumerable sycophants have vanished without a trace.

Samuel

"Samuel grew up and the Lord was with him, not permitting any word of his to be without effect". (1 Sam 3:19).

The figure of Samuel serves as an illustration and bridge from the experience of bands of ecstatic prophets to the individual persons remembered by name for their relationship (or hostility) to the royal house. As a sign of Samuel's importance in the eyes of the biblical writers, they include an account of his childhood by way of introduction. This is a unique tribute. It places Samuel beside Moses whose childhood in Egypt was remembered, even in the legendary form preserved at the beginning of the story of Exodus (Ex 1-2). Not even David's first years were deemed worthy of preservation. After Samuel's mother had received the promise of the Lord's favorable response to her prayers (1 Sam 1:17), the child was born and then dutifully dedicated to temple worship by his parents. This little lad's eager response to the call of God in the night remains a very touching story and a powerful paradigm. As he began, so did he mature, ever responsive to Yahweh who made him a prophet by fulfilling each word spoken by the young man in Eli's temple at Shiloh (3:19). He spanned the transition from high place to royal court.

Samuel functioned as the first legitimator of kings in Judah and Israel, and served as a conscience in their regard. He selected and anointed Saul as Captain (*nagid*; 1 Sam 10:1), then announced his rejection in favor of David whom he also anointed (16:13). Born of Hannah the Ephraimite, Samuel began his life as a child dedicated to service in the temple at Shiloh (1:1ff). As such he provides an important link with the earliest covenantal experience of those who banded together at the major shrines in the new land of Canaan. He also symbolizes the movements from sanctuary servant to political prophet. Upon his lips is placed the first formal announcement of the rejection of the priestly family of Eli (3:12-14).

It would be very profitable at this time to turn to the biblical text itself, and to experience again a leisurely, prayerful reading of the story of Samuel (1 Sam 1-3; 8-13; 15-16). Linger over the text to see what images or associations come to mind.

The early legends associated with Samuel insist on the

young boy's growth before the Lord (2:21.26). The same phrase was used by the Gospel of Luke to describe the personal development of John the Baptizer and Jesus in later New Testament times (Lk 1:80; 2:52). The shadow of Samuel fell far, always indicating new beginnings in vigorous and faithful response to the will of God. The description of Samuel as one who kept trying to listen to the mysterious voice of the Lord in the darkness of night provides a paradigm or model for the experience of many people. He was commanded to pray, "Speak, Lord, for your servant is listening!" (1 Sam 3:9). Samuel listened so carefully that his words were inevitably fulfilled and verified by God (3:19.21). Literally his name means "El (God) has listened" and he gave graphic illustration to the label by living his whole life in a reciprocal stance of open response to that same God.

Samuel invited his people to the worship of the Lord alone (7:3-4) and offered sacrifices to celebrate their union with their God (v. 9). He served as a "judge" in Israel, settling disputes and maintaining order within the community. In the face of danger he proclaimed a holy war against the Philistines. Contradictory traditions regarding Samuel's role in establishing the monarchy are interwoven side by side into the biblical text. One tradition suggests that the request of Israel for a human king was viewed by Samuel as a rejection of the Lord (8:7; 12:12.19). Another tradition described the selection of Saul in more positive terms as genuinely endorsed by God (10:24; 11:15). The different perspectives of subsequent ages are probably reflected in these contradictory assessments. In any case Samuel did in fact preside over the transition from judge to monarch in Israel. He fashioned new forms of leadership to meet new needs. Such is the task of the prophet through whom the Spirit speaks! When all was said and done,

Samuel was remembered as one who prayed for his people and taught them (12:22). Like all prophets he was loyal to God and, therefore, he rejected Saul for his disobedient offering of sacrifice (13:14). Samuel was a person who belonged to the Lord throughout his entire life (1:28) and lived in the Spirit all his days (7:17).

Several decades later, after David had brought to the nation a peace and unity which Saul had not been able to achieve, there was a struggle for succession to the throne. Zadok the priest joined Nathan the prophet in endorsing Solomon and in intervening to have him anointed king (1 K 1:8,44f). Once again the action illustrates the bond between the prophetic agent of the Spirit and political activism. A strict dualistic separation between religion and politics was never a temptation for Israel. The earliest known prophets demonstrated that bond by their action and established the pattern expected of all who follow in the authentic path of the Judaeo-Christian tradition. Faith has an inevitable effect on the political and social realm or it is not true faith.

Later kings sought out influential and respected prophetic figures for advice and for legitimation of their policies. The saintly Josiah, for example, sent a delegation to the prophetess Huldah for her judgment on the value of a scroll found during the restoration of the temple in 622 F.C.E. (2 K 22:14). This marked a major turning point for Judah as written revelation became the law of the land. A few decades later King Zedekiah kept asking Jeremiah in prison for his assessment of the Babylonian crisis even though the repeated response of the prophet was profoundly distressing to the king (Jer 37:17-20; 38:14-28). Some kings obeyed; some did not. The Word of God continued to govern the history of the people.

One of the geniuses of the Hebraic mentality and its sacred

literature is the practice of describing the beginning of virtually every major human institution or practice in glowing terms almost larger than life. Somehow beginnings and endings are important for what they reveal of the basic reality of things. The loving look at the origins of humanity in Genesis or the origins of Israel in Exodus are familiar examples of this custom. Those aspects were highlighted which emphasized the deepest nature of things.

No less is true of prophecy. Samuel stands out as a concrete illustration. In him we see a great deal of the history and purpose of prophecy as finally understood by those who wove together the ancient traditions and fashioned the inspired story of the first great prophet in Israel. The concern of later theologians is present in the selective sifting of many stories about Samuel. This encourages us to read carefully, asking repeatedly why such narratives were preserved. How did the stories continue to illustrate (and resolve) later dilemmas and questions? After all, it was the later questions which influenced the existing shape of the story.

A recent television play pictured the rejected and dejected Saul at the end of his life in bitter wonderment, sagely advising a colleague, "never let an old man pour oil on your head!" When it was all over, he wasn't so sure that he should have allowed Samuel to pour the oil of anointing upon his young head. This contemporary fantasy captured the role of prophet in Israel, somehow making and breaking kingly leaders by word and ritual, influencing history in God's name. Those who spoke boldly and acted decisively were remembered by name. Those who knew God better than their contemporaries are still venerated as persons of the Spirit. They insist on dwelling in the recesses of our memory. They possess a relation to the living God which continues to fascinate each generation because these prophets struggled with questions of enduring significance.

❧

Three echoes from the high place for future generations:

Where does religious experience occur today?

Which leadership figures can spark and sustain those experiences?

Is there any contemporary social or political alternative to which you can contribute your life and energy in a creative (and prophetic) fashion?

2

Most Zealous For The Lord

Among the most influential of the spirited prophets of Israel towers the figure of Elijah the Tishbite from the land of Gilead just east of the Jordan River (I K 17:1). He is presented as an individual woven into the theological legends and reminiscences of the Deuteronomic history (1 K 17—2 K 2). In fact, Elijah played a major role in the evolution of the religious traditions of Israel. In that age of syncretistic distractions and dangerous flirtation with the religious foundations of the political power in neighboring nations, Elijah stood tall and strong, firmly recalling the people of Israel to the life-giving core of their ancestral faith. It was an age of excessive and destructive pluralism, and Elijah could not be content without clearer lines and sharper moral imperatives. With the driving zeal of a reformer and the keen insight of a visionary, he took strong action to purify the royal house of the northern kingdom. The spirit rendered him an antagonist to the colorful figure of Jezebel and her husband Ahab of the house of Omri. A prayerful reading of the story of Elijah (1 Kg 17—2 K 2) will set the stage for our reflections.

The Elijah of history may not have been a very likeable personality, for the stamp of his harshness and the vigor of his uncompromising spirit rendered him a very uncomfortable person in the various ecumenical ventures of the 9th century

B.C.E. The legends concerning his life are fragmentary at best, but they leave no doubt as to the sharp edge of his convictions. While such figures may be the object of admiration more often than imitation, they perform in fact an invaluable service for the revitalization and living power of a religious tradition. The full impact of Yahwism was clarified by this zealous servant of a very jealous God who brooked neither rival nor compromise. Such human figures must be taken seriously in every age.

The political background begins with the shrewd strategy of king Omri who built a new capitol for the northern kingdom of Israel at Samaria (1 K 16:24) and encouraged close ties with the Phoenician cities to the north. His son Ahab continued the same policies, even marrying Jezebel, the daughter of the king of Sidon, and embracing her religious devotion to Baal. Being of the same practical and energetic bent as his father, Ahab went so far as to build a temple to Baal in Samaria (vv. 31-32)! It was enough to raise the hackles of any respectable prophet, and Elijah was equal to the challenge.

Jezebel and her advisors took Elijah and his colleagues so seriously that she began a pogrom of extermination, murdering many of the prophets of Yahweh as they were discovered (18:4.13). It must have been the spirit of the age, for when it was Elijah's turn to be at the top, he did some slitting of prophetic throats himself (18:40).

With the abruptness often characteristic of the truly charismatic leader, Elijah appeared in sharp contrast to his age. The text wastes no words in introducing him to the scene (17:1). Approximately a century after Solomon began his reign as master builder of the Temple and major fortifications in Israel and Judah, Elijah rose to reject the earlier importation of Phoenician religious ritual which had subtly accompanied the architectural skills of the builders. Those who refashioned Jerusalem according to the more sophisticated tastes of Solomon's foreign wives and their courts might have known something about construction, but their religious convictions were simply unacceptable to the prophet.

While Judah struggled in the south with the major implications of the heritage bequeathed by Solomon's more international interests, the northern kingdom of Israel experienced a remarkable economic growth under the astute leadership of King Omri (886-865 B.C.E.) and his son Ahab. As indicated above, they engaged in many successful commercial enterprises. These ventures enhanced the reputation of the nation in the eyes of surrounding royal dynasties. Unfortunately, they also increased the cultural influence of the nations (*go'im*) on the mores of the royal city of Samaria. Interdynastic marriages strengthened alliances and various religious rituals reenforced those bonds. The residue of Canaanite fertility practices in the towns of the north received new encouragement from the expectations of traveling merchants who presumed the presence of cult prostitutes as a means of assuring success and prosperity in their ventures. Whatever form advertising may have taken in the 9th century B.C.E., the fertility aspect of economic success would have been encouraged. Farmers in the Plain of Jezrael ritualized the fertility of the seasons to obtain favorable conditions and abundant harvests. It simply seemed like the right thing to do in their idea of "modern" farming! All these factors converged to provide an atmosphere which found the rigors of Yahwism difficult and demanding, certainly out of step with the age.

A slightly later age, perhaps during the 8th century B.C.E., witnessed the strong stirrings of the Deuteronomic reform movement with its vigorous monotheistic stance in a world populated by Canaanite deities. For those northern Deuteronomist theologians of the 8th century and their southern successors of the 7th and 6th centuries B.C.E., Elijah became the perfect spokesman for their deepest beliefs regarding the unique supremacy of Yahweh alone. In a similar manner Jeremiah became their voice in criticism of the worship in the Temple of Jerusalem. In formulating a theological explanation for the final fall of Israel before their Assyrian conquerors, these Deuteronomic historians attempted to summon Israel to a theological purity previously unknown (2 K 17:7-23). The memory of the reforming zeal of Elijah provided the perfect foil for such a pastoral project. In their eyes, it was the unmitigated resistance to the voice of the prophets which resulted in such social disaster. Somehow Elijah said it all.

Such is the need for heroes and heroines which even in our day takes good people like George Washington, Abraham Lincoln, or Martin Luther King and makes them even bigger than life for the sake of the movements they later serve. Similarly in the Church, saints are selected for the unique example they may provide for subsequent ages still struggling with old problems. Elizabeth Seton is a luminary for those confronted by issues of ecumenism today, or raising children or keeping a parochial school open or being the single parent of a large family. Isabel of Spain may have been a most holy woman and an astute leader in charting new paths of political life. She may even be a remarkable example for women entering new roles in government and society, but her alleged anti-Semitic views may be a bit much for the heightened sensitivities of our modern age some five hundred years later. It remains a question for the discerning community.

As the Deuteronomist theologians viewed things, they felt they needed to insist once more on the unicity of God. The pluralism of their age was simply too divisive and destructive. They unfurled the banner phrase which became the daily prayer of devoted Jews ever since, namely the profession of faith, "Hear O Israel! The Lord is our God, the Lord alone" (Dt 6:4). For these theological geniuses, it logically followed that there was but one election of one people called to a single response and a unique inheritance: one God, one people, one Torah, one Temple. For them the role of the king was simply to know revealed divine instruction and to represent the people before God. The prophet according to the Deuteronomist spoke the living word of God which governed the course of human history. From such singularity of purpose and meaning arose their strong polemic against all rivals and impostor deities.

Such was the Deuteronomic vision which served as a prism for the figure of Elijah. Formulated a century and a half after his death, their tradition remembered Elijah as a remarkable model for the zeal which should characterize all Yahweh's servants, especially those raised up by God to speak and execute his sovereign word. The figure of Elijah readily became a new Moses sent to reestablish the purity of Israel's faith in an age which had lost the sharp distinctions of its earlier radical response to an uncompromising God.[1]

Prophetic legends regarding powerful figures like Elijah were not newly created by the Deuteronomists. Memories of isolated concrete events were gathered over the years by the various bands of disciples which formed around more outstanding charismatic figures, just as bands of men and women gathered around saintly abbots in the desert during the first

---

[1] For a classic study, see H.H. Rowley, "Elijah on Mount Carmel," *Men of God* (Nelson, 1963) 37-65.

centuries of Christianity. In each of the stories was the nucleus of a divine message. The particular teaching or revelation was rooted in the historical reality of that moment, but well worth recalling for application elsewhere because of its impact or perception. Sometimes a symbolic action captured the intent of the prophet's meaning and was remembered, as for example, the seemingly endless supply of food from the generous widow's oil jug and flour jar in time of need (1 K 17:7-16). It was Yahweh alone who fed the world!

Small collections on a theme, such as the vivid power of the prophet's word (1 K 17:1-24), were also undoubtedly recounted in these prophetic groups. Through later lenses, however selective, the figure of Elijah, "most zealous for the Lord, the God of hosts' (19:10) was preserved and sharpened for the benefit of subsequent generations.

A Person Of Burning Loyalty And Zeal

"I have been most jealous for the Lord, the God of hosts, but the Israelites have forsaken your covenant, torn down your altars, and put your prophets to the sword. I alone am left and they seek to take my life" (1 Kg 19:10).

Jealousy is a basic human emotion which finds expression in many areas of life. The Hebrew word *qana'* which literally means "be red or glow," hence, "be suffused with the emotion of envy or jealousy," is the term in question. Since the word is listed among the seven capital sins of Christianity, it may be surprising to learn that it was one of the early titles of God! Embedded in one of the earlier layers of the Decalogue is the acknowledgement of *El Qana'*, the "Jealous God" ever "inflicting punishment for their fathers' wickedness on the children of those who hate me, down to the third and fourth generations, but bestowing mercy (*hesed*) down to the thousandth generation on the children of those who love me and keep my commands' (Ex 20:5-6; Dt 5:9-10; cf 6:15).

Since the term and title is preserved in this initial and very ancient section of the Decalogue, it must have represented a significant element in the history of the religious tradition. Students of biblical theology often lament the fact that a very truncated version of the Decalogue was taught to christian children over the years. While this catechetical practice may have been simpler, it resulted in an impoverished notion of the God of Israel's love for the faithful members of the divine family.

To apply such an emotion as "jealousy" to God in an anthropomorphic fashion is, in fact, to stress the profoundly personal and relational nature of Yahweh. This was a God venerated for his strong sense of possessive care for the people of his covenant, and also for his vigorous defense of their needs in the face of enemies and rivals. The concept demands a certain moral exclusivity which sets Yahweh apart from the forces of natural fertility. If pushed too far by human weakness or capriciousness, this God will insist on his rights and may even vindicate those rights. The moral stipulations of the covenant and the responses expected from Israel take on the character of being non-negotiables in life.

Zeal for the cause of Yahweh marked Elijah's life as recorded in the First Book of Kings. Like Joshua before him (Jos 24:19-21), Elijah insisted that the people make a clear commitment to Yahweh, for both of these leaders understood the possible anger of One lightly cast aside for the gods of the nations (1 K 18:21). Like Phinehas, son of Eleazar, son of Aaron the priest, whose jealousy for Yahweh's honor led him to kill a flagrantly sinning Israelite and his Midianite concubine

(Nm 25:10-13), Elijah wielded his angry sword against the four hundred and fifty prophets of Baal attached to the court of Jezebel (1 K 18:40). Such leaders were not afraid to make a decision in faith, to demand a response from others, nor to enforce perseverance in that commitment. They could see no alternative if integrity was to be preserved.

In view of such deep convictions and forceful energy, it should not be surprising to see Elijah described as a person marked by abruptness and charismatic spontaneity. The very clarity of his single-minded response to Yahweh led him to immediate conclusions in reference to proper worship and acceptable moral conduct. It may have been that very quality which the inspired editors desired to highlight by suddenly introducing Elijah into the midst of the religious aberration fostered by Ahab, the new King of Israel (1 K 16:29-17:1).

Whether Elijah was a person of ecstatic vision similar to the prophet Micaiah ben Imlah (1 K 22:19-23), or simply one who remained constantly conscious of the burning reality of God, he is quoted as describing himself as intimately related to Yahweh "before whom I stand" (17:1; 18:15). That same God responded by sending ravens to bring him food in the wilderness. Though ravens were considered unclean animals according to later Mosaic calculations (Nm 11:15), they were purified by their very service to the great prophet. Perhaps the text wishes to emphasize that Elijah saw a deeper goodness than was visible to the teachers and moralists of the later code of ritual purity which clarified the dietary prescription for post-exilic Judaism. Each morning and evening the ravens brought "bread and flesh" (1 K 17:4-6), clearly even outshining the generosity of Obediah a loyal servant of Yahweh in Ahab's court who hid prophets from the anger of Jezebel, but was only able to provide bread and water for them (18:13).

Bearer Of The Word

"'Now indeed I know that you are a man of God,' the woman replied to Elijah. 'The word of God comes truly from you.'" (1 K 17:24)

From the very beginning Elijah is presented as a person open to the *Dabar-YHWH*, "the word/event of God" (17:2.8.16.24; 18:1; 19:9; 21:17.29). For Elijah and for the entire Deuteronomic tradition, the divine decree was at the very center of all history, personal as well as communal. An individual was viewed as the concrete expression of the entire community. All were subject to the powerful word of God in all things.

Inspired by God's word, Elijah announced a drought as punishment for the fertility cult promoted by Ahab and as graphic demonstration of the true source of fertility in Israel (17:1). The same word led him to bless the generosity of the starving widow whose jar of flour and jug of oil did not fail throughout the entire famine (vv. 7-16). This was the material blessing of Yahweh extended to the needy who unselfishly care for his prophets. Similarly, the word enabled Elijah to restore the widow's son to life (vv. 17-24), vindicating the prophet as a person of God.

Again it was God's word which led Elijah to his famous ritual confrontation with the prophets of Baal on Mount Carmel (18:21-46). In the context of that sacrifice, he summoned the long awaited rains by his announcement and by the ritual pouring of water on the offerings. Although at first glance it might seem that water was used to make the burning more difficult and the test more impressive, its connection as a prophetic action related to the rain should not be overlooked.

In this context the water also served as the first drops of the God-given torrent which shortly occured over the entire land, bringing the terrible drought to an end.

The fire of Yahweh which consumed the prophet's sacrifice (18:38) demonstrated the reality of Yahweh and his word in Israel. It also vindicated Elijah's ministry and unleashed the fury of Jezebel (19:2). Such is the price one may be forced to pay when associated with the power of God active in human history.

Fire was a very appropriate symbol for the divine presence: immaterial, illuminating, purifying, warming, burning, moving and, therefore, alive. Whether consuming a sacrifice on Mount Carmel or domesticated into a sanctuary lamp in the Temple, (Ex 25:31-40; 27:20-21), fire reminded everyone of the presence and power of God in the world. That this should occur at the behest of Elijah indicated both the power of the prophet's speech and the close relationship to the Lord which he enjoyed. Even the presence of divine fire was the result of the word of Elijah.

The message of loyal prophets is never isolated from the stuff of human life; consequently it is often presented in symbolic actions which both illustrate the communication and initiate the reality so portrayed. Ritual sacrifice expresses obedience to Yahweh, but so also does the anointing of Hazael as King of Aram (Syria) and the prophetic designation of Jehu as King of Israel in place of Ahab (19:15-16). The world of political power was intimately related to the theocracy in which Israel's prophets lived. When Elijah cast his mantle over the shoulders of Elisha as an indication of the legitimate succession in prophetic authority, the word was made concrete and effective (19:19). From such dramatic encounters the legends grew and flourished.

Guardian Of Mosaic Tradition

"Then, strengthened by that food, he walked forty days and forty nights to the mountain of God, Horeb." (1 K 19:8)

Elijah was no innovator in the history of Israel's faith; rather he forced his contemporaries to recall the burning focus of their ancestor's faith. To underscore his commitment to tradition, the Deuteronomic historians presented him as sharing some of the same experiences as those who had left Egypt under the leadership of Moses some four hundred years earlier. It was in the wilderness of Transjordanian territory, beside Wadi Kerith, that Elijah lived during the drought (17:3). It was to the wilderness of Beer-sheba in his haste to avoid the burning anger of Jezebel after the murder of her prophets that he fled (19:3). Like Moses fleeing the anger of the Pharaoh after the murder of the Egyptian (Ex 2:15), Elijah took refuge in the wilderness on his way to Horeb. There he was fed in his despair and provided with strength and purpose for his journey of forty days and forty nights to Horeb, the Mountain of God (19:8).

Like Moses who begged to see the face of God on Sinai again after the sin of his people and the destruction of the golden calf (Ex 33:18-34:9), Elijah was also blessed for his zealous service (1 K 19:10) and granted a mysterious moment in the presence of God. In contrast to the experience of Moses, that powerful God was not encountered in wind, earthquake or fire, but rather in a tiny whispering sound (vv. 11-12). The Hebrew phrase translated as a "whispering sound" or "still small voice" has remained itself mysterious and controverted among all subsequent generations of biblical interpreters. Literally the words suggest something thinly beaten or ground into silent dust. Was it a rejection of the violence used by Elijah in his dealings with the prophets of Baal? Was it God's manner of insisting that deepest revelation is found in more ordinary events of daily life? Perhaps the phrase's perennial resistance to clear explanation provides the humbling balance necessary to prevent zealous servants from becoming self-righteous before God! The thought makes us pause for a moment to take note of the unexpected way in which God seems to speak most effectively to us in our own contemporary lives.

The Mosaic tradition was not only identified with flight from despotic royalty or theophanies in the desert, it also stressed the bond of covenant which commanded mutual care between the members, especially for widows and orphans as examples of people in the direst of need. Elijah's presence brought food and renewed life to the desperate widow of Zarephath, a town in Phoenician territory some seven miles south of Sidon. That act was evidence of Mosaic solicitude for the needy, even those living outside the territory of Israel, just as Moses had cared for the daughters of Jethro in Midianite territory (Ex 2:15-19). Similarly the intervention of Elijah in the shabby treatment and murder of Naboth whose vineyard was obtained by Ahab in gross violation of Mosaic legislation (1 K 21:1-24) reinforced the image of Elijah as one who upheld the covenant and cared for God's people.

Every faith generation remembers what it needs in order to survive as a people of unity and purpose.

Confronter Of Kings

"'Have you found me out, my enemy?' Ahab said to Elijah. 'Yes,' he answered, 'because you have given yourself up to doing evil in the Lord's sight'" (1 K 21:20).

Because in the judgment of Elijah no human being had merit except when zealously serving Yahweh, faithless kings and rulers were addressed without pity or compassion. The close bond between the politics and religion of his day resulted in Elijah's reputation as a relentless foe and enemy of the royal house, a "disturber of Israel" as Ahab labeled him in one of their more memorable meetings (18:17)! The economic and political prestige of the Omride dynasty, verified by archaeology and diplomatic correspondence from neighboring nations, meant nothing to Elijah or his Deuteronomic biographers, for they could think of nothing except the fact that Ahab had abandoned the commands of Yahweh (18:18), and, therefore, deserved to be rejected together with his entire family line from his throne. Moreover, the judgment uttered by Elijah indicated that this downfall would occur in such a violent manner that the dogs would lick his blood from the very spot where the King had caused the blood of Naboth to be spilled (21:19)!

Prophet and political activist were one and the same thing for these early messengers of Yahweh the God of armies. The very title "God of hosts/armies (*saba'oth*)" may either refer to the stars of heaven believed to be God's military troops, or may have been a majestic plural title better translated as "Great Warrior." The title was used by Elijah, when he spoke of the powerful leader to whom the prophet was pledged (20:10). In the eyes of Elijah all human kings ruled at the pleasure of Yahweh and were often speedily dismissed by prophetic figures, sometimes in great blood baths for the nation. Dynasties tumbled one after another in the northern kingdom and the power of prophets was awesome. While such a state of affairs provided at times a type of check and balance between very real human powers, it also afforded the opportunity for disposing of rivals in the name of God without respect for individual rights (as moderns would view it) or care for possibly mistaken judgment. Untempered religious zeal can be ruthless, as history attests all too often.

Those who are troubled by the mentality or political activism of neo-conservative Moslem groups today, and those who find it difficult to understand the supreme authority of figures such as the Ayatollah Khomeini, might benefit from studying Elijah. There truly seems to be a clear parallelism between their desperate attempts to purify their contemporary culture from various alien and wicked influences from the West and similar efforts initiated by Elijah and his reformers some three millennia ago. Those who respect the accomplishments of Elijah in ancient Israel should understand the fact that similar hopes are the motivation of some of the more extreme fundamentalist leaders in the Near East today. Religious fanaticism in any tradition becomes acceptable to their followers in direct proportion to the desperateness of their cause or the fear that essential values could be lost without drastic action. Such comparisons may be unwelcome, but they serve to dramatize and contemporize the issues faced by Elijah. They also serve to illustrate the enduring reality posed by religious zeal and passion. False prophets are destroyed when they pose such a threat that their mere presence cannot be tolerated. Those who take the judgment of God in hand need to recognize the two-edged sword in their grasp, usually wounding the hand which wields it. Anyone who speaks of a different god is viewed as a false prophet by someone!

This only confirms the fact that religious and prophetic faith always has some impact on the political sphere and disturbs the status quo of those in power.

Followers And Agents

"Elijah said to Elisha, 'Ask for whatever I may do for you before I am taken from you.' Elisha answered, 'May I receive a double portion of your spirit.' 'You have asked for something that is not easy,' he replied. 'Still, if you see me taken up from you, your wish will be granted.'" (2 K 2:9-10)

Even the mighty Elijah could not accomplish everything alone, and consequently Elisha was designated as successor for the anointing of kings. He was also chosen for the task of leading the seven thousand (19:18) who remained loyal to Yahweh under the duress of seductive culture and reprisals from the royal house. At the very end of their association, Elisha asked for a "double portion" of Elijah's spirit as a sign that he was recognized as eldest son according to Israel's laws of inheritance (Dt 21:17). In the last analysis, however, the gift of the spirit is God's to give alone, and God distributes that spirit as God chooses, showing favor to whomever God wills (Ex 33:19). Elijah's exit in a fiery chariot marked his departure from history as recorded by the Deuteronomists. Loyal and zealous to the end, he was caught up into the fiery presence of Yahweh as a sign of divine approval and blessing (2 K 2:1-18).

On three occasions as Elijah and Elisha journeyed to the site of Elijah's destined encounter with his God, they met prophetic groups who seemed to have foreknowledge of Elijah's imminent departure. These prophetic communities may be among the very groups which collected and cherished stories about Elijah and his wonder-working disciple Elisha. The power of God encompassed this singular servant and carried him to unknown realms. In fact it may have been complete ignorance of his final resting place which inspired the dramatic account of his departure. With legendary details embroidered upon the fabric of Elijah's end, the biblical text illustrates the blessing given by God to all who serve him with generosity and singleness of heart.

The description of Elisha picking up the mantle of Elijah which had fallen from the chariot in the final whirlwind of fire (2:13) suggests that those who recalled this account of the transfer of authority were not the same as those who described Elijah casting his cloak over the shoulders of a plowing Elisha (1 K 19:19). The mantle was the issue and the way authority was transferred in fact varied from one account to another. Each story was treasured by some community. The bond between Scripture and communities of faith continues to be verified on so many levels! Moreover, the importance of material symbols and human ritual for designating those called to lead a community of faith seems to stand out. Each community, with an inner logic known only to itself, selects the item which speaks most directly. A mantle certainly evoked the notion of all-encompassing and supporting divine presence.

Though sufficiently irascible in his own right, even to the point of summoning angry bears to maul the little boys who mocked his baldness (2 K 2:23-25), Elisha was more remembered for the various wonders he performed. Like his master, Elisha also multiplied a widow's oil, this time to preserve her and her family from hard-hearted creditors (4:1-7) and brought a widow's child back to life (vv. 8-37). He miraculously fed the hungry (vv. 42-44); he also brought healing and Yahwistic faith to Naaman the Syrian (5:1-19). He announced an end to the dreadful famine at Samaria (6:24-7:20) and in that context restored land to a poor widow, again demonstrating the Mosaic roots of his faith and power. The God of Moses always give liberty to slaves and land to the dispossessed. Elisha's own loyalty to all the consequences of the Mosaic covenant makes him a worthy disciple who seems a bit more human than Elijah in fulfilling the inexorable demands of God's word to Israel.

Divine And Human Zeal

"The zeal of the Lord of hosts will do this" (Is 9:6).

Elijah and Elisha were not the only prophets marked by a zeal for the Lord. All the classical prophets, that is, those whose pronouncements were preserved in some written form, possessed an urgency regarding the Lord they served. Amos was driven by an inner power to journey northwards in order to denounce Israelite worshipers at the royal sanctuary for their callousness toward the poor (Am 2:6-8).

In another situation, with all the conviction of a dedicated modern pacifist, Isaiah attempted to halt the foolish preparations for war in Jerusalem (Is 7:3; 31:1). In what may have been an oracle composed to celebrate the birth of prince Hezekiah, son of Ahaz, Isaiah described the end of war by the burning of blood-soaked battle uniforms for fuel (7:4). He also announced the commencement of a totally peaceful reign and confidently assured the royal cabinet that "the zeal of the Lord of hosts will do this" (v. 6)!

The text repeats the very same phrase when Hezekiah himself is confronted by the imminent invasion of the Assyrian king Sennacherib in 701 B.C.E. It was the historic moment celebrated in Lord Byron's classic poem which recalled that "The Assyrian came down down like a wolf on the fold, and his cohorts were gleaming in purple and gold." The troops were gathered about the city walls of Jerusalem while dialogue and threats were exchanged between the encampments (2 K 18:13-19:37). The prophet Isaiah encouraged trust and confidence in the protective power of the Lord for his chosen Zion, for again the Lord's zeal would accomplish its purpose (Is 37:32). The next morning, whether by miraculous divine intervention or plague, some hundred and eighty-five thousand Assyrian troops were struck down and the king went home (vv. 33-37). From confidence in the Lord's power came prophetic courage and zeal. The humanity of the prophet was but a shadow of the divine in zealous pursuit of peace.

The prophet Nahum celebrated the fall and destruction of the hated city of Nineveh and exulted in the annihilation of that dreadful site. The Assyrians had been the "Nazis" of their day and Nahum could hardly restrain his delight in the final judgment of the Lord upon that nation. Divine zeal and prophetic zeal meshed in Nahum's poetic description of the end of the great capital (Nah 1-3). It was 613 B.C.E. and the trust of Isaiah finally found fulfillment in the punishment meted out to the Assyrians. At least that's the way Nahum saw it.

The anger of people like Elijah and Nahum makes us nervous, for we have been trained to offer compassion to our enemies as well as any judgment rightly deserved. The book of Nahum clearly stands in almost complete contradiction to the story of the prophet Jonah who went to Nineveh, albeit unwillingly, and there discovererd a people open to the Word of God and ready for conversion! The actual inner attitude of the human figure of Jonah is in fact rather close to the spirit of Nahum, and the God of Jonah would seem to stand in judgment of both. Like Nahum, however, Jonah didn't seem to believe that the Ninevites deserved a chance. Nahum begins his oracles with a resounding defense of divine judgment against the wicked and follows with a graphic description of the sounds and sights of the final battle against Nineveh. The Lord is described as "a jealous and avenging God" (1:1), using the traditional formulas of familiar oracles against the nations to assert Yahweh's supremacy over all the world, for he "never leaves the guilty unpunished" (v. 3). Is there ever a place for relentless righteous anger in the larger scheme of things? Has Nahum caught a spark from Elijah's fiery chariot? How much zeal is too much? Is an angry and zealous God less a God? If jealousy brooks no rivals or compromises in principle, can it ever tolerate the arrogance of injustice or violence against God's faithful people? Does error have any rights? The last question had never even been conceived by Elijah nor by those who continued to exercise zeal in the name of the Lord. The prophetic stance of Nahum was correct, and the poetry compelling, but he didn't represent the whole truth. He needed the author of the book of Jonah to add the necessary reminder that divine zeal was for peace in its most profound sense, namely the reintegration of people into a just and faithful society. Maybe Nahum knew it, but just gave up a bit sooner than the Lord he served. Students of the larger horizon of biblical revelation are not only instructed by the parable of Jonah, which was probably written a century or two later, but also by the fact that an even later Galilean Prophet chose the village of Capharnaum (literally Village of Nahum) as a base of operations for preaching a Kingdom of mercy and justice for all. In the long run, things do balance out!

Only a few years later the prophet Habakkuk seems to have turned his zeal against the Babylonians, that "bitter and unruly people" (Hab 1:6) who marched across the middle

East, scoffing at kings and laughing at all enemy fortresses (v. 10). Habakkuk knew that the divine zeal would inevitably hit its just mark; so he cautioned patience, "For the vision still has its time, presses on to fulfillment and will not disappoint" (2:3). It was a wise bit of advice for those who struggle under the crushing burden of oppression and violence. The anger of Habakkuk was directed against the human rights violation of the foreign nations who stored up what was not their own (v. 6), pursued evil again for themselves (v. 9), built cities by bloodshed (v. 12), and gave their neighbors a flood of wrath to drink (v. 15). To all who suffered such cruelty, Habakkuk counseled patience, for the vision will surely come; "it will not be late" (v. 3). The enduring consolation of Habakkuk's message is found in his observation that "the just man, because of his faith, shall live" (v. 4). It was Habakkuk's contribution to leave an explicit reminder for God's people, namely that reality, the zeal of God, was in the service of those who are truly faithful.

Zephaniah turned his attention upon the evils of the temple in Jerusalem and promised a terrible destruction when the Day of the Lord would finally come. In words which would become part of the great Christian lament, the *Dies Irae*, Zephaniah described the day of the Lord which would mark the zealous anger of God against his own people for their infidelity (Zeph 1:15). Zephaniah saw a temple ritual in dire need of profound liturgical reform, with focus on the inner spirit as well external ritual. Whether he was among those supporting the proposed reforms of Josiah or citicizing their inadequacy during the latter decades of the seventh century B.C.E., he railed against "all who leap over the threshold, who fill the house of their master with violence and deceit" (Zeph 1:9). The counsel of Zephaniah is directed to "all you humble

('anawim) of the earth, who have observed his law" (2:3),
adding a remarkable oracle in the Lord's name: "I will leave as
a remnant in your midst a people humble and lowly, who shall
take refuge in the name of the Lord" (3:12). With growing
clarity the prophets realized that the zeal of the Lord was at
the service of those who knew the true nature of their
dependence on God's power. In order to protect and liberate
the Lord's faithful and humble people, it was necessary to
invoke the righteous anger of God. For that reason Zephaniah
looked forward to the Day of the Lord "when in the fire of his
jealousy all the earth shall be consumed" (1:18; 3:8).

One of the recurring themes in pre-exilic prophecy is the
Day of the Lord. Images of power are gathered to describe a
final intervention from the Lord whose jealous anger erupts in
behalf of the people and against their oppressors. Because the
theme seems to be primarily one of salvation rather than
judgment, it will be treated in that context, even though these
three "minor prophets" are very closely associated with the
imminent Day of the Lord.

Jeremiah, roughly a contemporary of Nahum, Habakkuk
and Zephaniah, also had to proclaim the destruction of the
Temple he loved, and did so with fire in his eyes as well as in
his bones (Jer 7:1-15; 20:9). His qualification led to the
promise of a new covenant (31:31-34), but the angry promise
of judgment against those who misused the presence of the
Lord in temple worship hovered over his entire life. A sense of
urgency, some spark of passion, marks all who are loyal to a
cause. Anyone committed to God and his will experiences that
burning edge along some issue of life in God's world. Each
prophet experienced that zeal in the concrete circumstances of
his or her own life. Even after the Exile when prophets
encouraged the rebuilding of the temple, the theme of zeal

returned to provide motivation and courage in the words of the Lord through Zechariah, "I am intensely jealous for Zion, stirred to jealous wrath for her" (Zech 8:2). Through all of history, Elijah remains as a figure especially marked with that quality. He was indeed remembered as one who was always "most zealous for the Lord" (1 K 19:10)

It remains one of the curiosities of Scriptures that the reputation of Elijah, so starkly presented in the accounts of his prophetic activity, changed drastically over the centuries. In later ages Elijah was invoked as the one who would bridge generations, converting parents and children to each other once more (Mal 3:23). Perhaps it was the power of his conviction which enabled Elijah to become an image of restoration for later prophets when another culture, this time Persian in nature, was active in seducing the leadership of Jerusalem from purity of worship and covenanted loyalty. The memory of a prophet through later generations is a very plastic reality, capable of being remolded according the the needs of each age. Elijah was single-hearted and single-minded. He was driven to fidelity. A new age might provide a new purpose, but the energy inspired by fidelity remained the same.

☙

Three crusts of bread from Elijah's ravens for future generations to chew over:

Are we truly zealous about anything of value today?

Are there any lines in areas of justice or faith

beyond which no compromise is ever possible in life?

When was the last time we became angry enough to do something simply because we knew it was right?

3

Creative Call And Election

The God of Israel was not isolated in splendor, separate from the forces of creation or the upheavals of history, and neither were the prophets. Yahweh was God's name, a verb not a noun, and the word reflects the mysterious vitality of God's being.

It is difficult for us to imagine anyone truly called by a verb! The closest we come is an occasional nickname like "Skip" or "Buzz;" even the name of the contemporary movie actress, Whoopi Goldberg, is in fact an exclamation, not a verb. Israel, however, enjoyed calling people by verb forms. Remember how Father-of-a-Multitude (Abram) and Princess (*Sarah*) named their son He(God)-will-Listen (Ishmael)? The name, Israel itself is both fascinating and profound. The Hebrew root *sarah* means "to put things in order, to lead, to rule or to be a warrior." Once more the patriarch and the entire nation is called by a verb which means El(God)-will-rule (Israel). The very name is an expression of subordination and obedience to the Lord of the Covenant.

The God of Israel was venerated as one charged with life and power and was so called, even though the exact meaning of the sacred title "YHWH" continues to elude scholars. Perhaps the sacred name should be understood as an imperfect or future form of the verb *hwh*, (to be). In that sense the name would be interpreted as "He-Will-Be (whatever he will be)." This translation would serve as a recognition of God's constantly unfolding presence to each successive generation's needs. Other scholars prefer to see the word as a causative form of the verb which would then be more accurately translated as "He-Will-Make-Come-into-Being (Whatever will exist)" for it is YHWH alone who creates and sustains all things. The manner of writing the Divine Name which has recently become popular, namely Yahweh, presumes the causative explanation and supplies vowels accordingly. In any event, the God of Israel is deeply related to the world in which we live as the Source of Life.

The name itself became so sacred as a symbol of the Person of God that eventually it was never uttered except by the High Priest alone at the annual celebration of the Feast of the Atonement. Other names were used in prayer such as Adonai which means "My Great Lord". Even today the Name receives great respect among the Jewish people and an abbreviation is often used rather than the Name itself. Members of the Jewish community often protest against the cavalier use of the word "God" on coins which are saved in sundry improbable locations or used for unseemly purposes at times. This type of respect remains a lesson and a caution for all of us.

When the Lord touches the world, all of creation also becomes transformed, charged with new life and directed toward God's purposes. From chaos and confusion comes the world of night and day, the seasons for growth and the living chain of creatures crowned by Adam and Eve who dominated the world (Gen 1:20) by impressing their likeness upon it. They share the likeness of God by their creative imagination and lavish generosity in helping to put the world in order.

They image God by evoking the best from every creature. They and their descendants unite the world by directing its creatures to new purposes.

Some Calls Change Everything

"You alone have I favored, more than all the families of the earth" (Am 3:2).

The Lord of Israel has a special relationship to the prophets, weak human beings summoned by God in all their fragility. Their very frailty enables the success of their mission to be clearly seen as the work of the Lord of History alone. In their bond with Yahweh, the prophets often represented and typified all of Israel. Elijah was summoned from an unknown past to be zealous in his fidelity when few others thought it mattered very much. As a result of that call, Elijah climbed Mount Horeb and experienced the passage of God who transformed his weariness of spirit and sent him to anoint kings (1 K 19:9-18). In a too casual ecumenical age, Elijah insisted on gathering twelve stones to represent the covenant on Mount Carmel (18:31) for he alone remained and preserved the bond with the Lord of the Covenant (19:10,14).

Amos was merely a shepherd and dresser of sycamore trees (Am 7:14), perhaps associated with a sanctuary's flock or garden, but surely not a professional prophet by his own admission. He was called from the southern regions of Judah, suffused with the courage and anger of God in behalf of the poor, and sent to the holy place of Bethel in the north to announce the death of King Jeroboam (7:11) and the destruction of that venerable ancient sanctuary and its people

(9:1-8). Those suddenly outraged by a new insight into the unfairness of things will feel some of the fresh raw anger of Amos.

Hosea was told to marry Gomer, a temple prostitute, and to make his troubled marriage a sign and symbol of God's anguished love for his faithless people Israel (Hos 1:2). The life of Hosea was bitter at times and heart-wrenching as his own human fidelity and tender love became an expression of the Lord's call to renounce the seductive fertility rites of the age. Those who remain single after a broken marriage understand the cost of Hosea's witness and also something of the transforming power of God needed to sustain that witness each day.

Isaiah became dreadfully conscious of his sinful speech as he stood before the mysterious presence of the Lord in the Temple (Is 6:5). Suddenly all he could think of was his self-serving words in court or the completely unacceptable taste of all his prior prattle about the ways of God. The description of Isaiah's call includes some type of symbolic cleansing of his lips with a burning coal as a purification before being sent to proclaim a message which his own people would not be able to understand (vv. 9-10). Anyone who has ever been filled with remorse over things said in anger or teasing will also know regret that the words had ever been spoken and will recognize the self-punishment of wishing one's mouth could be washed out and cleansed again. As a result of his transformation, Isaiah lived with a vibrant sense of God's glory which fills heaven and earth, uniting both realms forever! Through that experience Isaiah learned to trust the Lord thoroughly and he invited others to follow suit even if he knew they would never do so (30:15-18).

Jeremiah was perhaps the prime example of a prophet

called and transformed. He had the conviction that from his mother's womb he had always been set apart, "sanctified" in that sense, and destined for the prophetic vocation (Jer 1:5). The Hebrew word for "holy" is *quadosh*, which means "set apart" or "separated" in some manner from common ordinary use. From an uncertain young lad of about eighteen he became a confronter of princes and kings, and a veritable wall of brass against the leaders of Jerusalem (v. 18). Lest anyone think such change is instant and painless, Jeremiah's story remains a consolation and encouragement, for he spoke bitter words against his Lord in a fit of depression. Jeremiah accused the Lord of seduction and treachery (with words charged with sexual undertones and familiar to his contemporaries from trials for rape; see 20:7). The only thing he heard by way of response was the relentless call to separate the truly valuable items from the trash of life, for God would strengthen and deliver him in the end (15:10-21). Constantly confronted by the smooth reassurances of other prophets who proclaimed a vastly different message, Jeremiah was deeply troubled by the announcement of destruction which he was compelled to proclaim. He only knew that he himself had stood in the council room of the Lord, and therefore understood what he had to say (23:16-40). His words became vigorous biting denunciations, hardly the simpering phrases of a lad too young to speak! Once more, like so many of the pre-exilic prophets, the call of the Lord had made the difference.

Each prophet knew his own weakness as would any discerning and honest person. Each prophet brought that soul-sized profile of cowardice and weakness into the presence of the Lord of the covenant. Some like Isaiah shrank before the burning purity of Yahweh. Others like Jeremiah or Ezekiel eagerly devoured the new message as if they were starving persons at a rich holiday banquet (Jer 15:16; Ez 3:1-3). The latter two were both subsequently asked to bear a heavy burden. Each was then remembered as a person of faith who had encountered the will of the Living God and survived to speak of it. Because Elijah struggled with the creative power of faith on Carmel and Horeb he was called "man of God (*ish-ha'elohim*)" (2 K 1:9.11.13) and conversely the Lord is described as "the God of Elijah" (2:14). A bond was created between them by the call and the response. Following the custom of the age, prophets often bore the very name of God in the shortened form of *"Yah"* or *"Yahu"* as one of the syllables of their own name. This also became a sign of the special bond between the Lord and his prophet. Among these are people like Elijah, Isaiah, Micah, Zephaniah and Jeremiah, while the name of Ezekiel includes a reference to the more generic divine title of "El (God)." Image what it would be like to live with so sacred a personal name! Do Hispanics with the name "Jesus" feel any disconcerting sentiments at the sound of their name, even when it's only a call to supper?

Those who received a difficult task in their meeting with the Lord, also received the strength and courage to accomplish it. Like Jeremiah they were promised protection and deliverance (Jer 1:8.19; 15:20) and sometimes that very promise was all they had to hang on to in the dark night of life!

Ezekiel was perhaps the strongest voice for the transformation which only God could achieve. After the destruction of the city of Jerusalem, living in exile, Ezekiel promised a new spirit and a new heart to the nation (Ez 11:19; 36:24-30). He also spoke of the transforming call and gift of the spirit to the dry dead bones of the nation (37:1-14). It was a creative call which promised that God would not allow a final "dead end" for his chosen people, not even that of exile which they had created for themselves by their sin.

A Covenantal Bond

"I will say to Lo-ammi, 'You are my people,' and he shall say, 'My God!'" (Hos 2:25).

Each of the pre-exilic prophets entered into a personal covenant with Yahweh. Not something as flimsy as a parchment agreement or a deal sealed by ritual handshake, the covenant was rather a deep abiding relationship between persons. Almost all Ancient Near Easter covenants contained or implied the same basic elements.[1] There was a sense of peace (*shalom*), reunited wholeness and renewed integrity between the partners of the covenant. By virtue of the covenant they were bound to exercise merciful fidelity (*hesed*), reciprocal kindness and concern, toward each other. They had in fact become members of the same family. Each covenant produced such restored peace, loyal fidelity and unity. Even political treaties between nations were phrased in terms of peace, mercy and family unity! Material blessing flowed from this bond of faith and unity. Obligations toward each other were also established by the covenant. When Yahweh became a gracious member of the covenant, these blessings and obligations were foundations for existence itself. When the human partner was a prophet called to serve the community, the

---

[1]For additional background in covenantal theology and Ancient Near Eastern literary forms, see the following: K. Balzer, *The Covenant Formulary* (Fortress, 1971); W. Beyerlin, *Origins and History of the Oldest Sinaitic Traditions* (Blackwell, 1965); D. Hillers, *Covenant: The History of a Biblical Idea* (John Hopkins, 1969); D. McCarthy, *Treaty and Covenant;* rev. ed. (Pontifical Biblical Institute, 1978); Idem, *The Old Testament Covenant: A Survey of Current Opinions* (John Knox Press, 1972); E. Nickolson, *Exodus and Sinai in History and Tradition* (John Knox Press, 1973); and R. Sklba, "The Redeemer of Israel," *Catholic Biblical Quarterly* 34 (1972) 3-17.

covenant bond contained challenge and support for the prophet. The Lord became present to the prophet and the prophet was recreated by that meeting.

It is easy to see in each prophetic dance with the Lord a miniature portrait of the entire nation's transforming calling. In Amos' condemnation of Israel, the Judean prophet from Tekoa stood in the courtyard of the royal sanctuary at Bethel and recalled the history of God's dealings with them. Amos reminded his audience of the fact that the Lord had brought them out of Egypt through the desert, destroyed the Amorite nation before them and raised up prophets and Nazarites (consecrated people like Samson; see Jgs 13:2-24) from their midst (Am 2:9-11). These leaders were symbols of the entire people. As such, they represented the close bond which the Lord had established with his people. Their response in faith was the measure of what was expected of all. Israel was conscious of being specially favored, more than any other nation (Am 3:2), which made their punishment inevitable when they walked away. Although other nations had been divinely guided in their massive migrations, such as the Philistines from Caphtor (Crete) or the Arameans from Kir (Mesopotamia), the eyes of the Lord were on Israel in a unique fashion and strict accountability was demanded of them (9:7-8).

While Amos may have been inclined to speak of the special relationship between Yahweh and Israel in terms of social responsibility, Hosea chose to use family imagery from the marital union. The exact historical circumstances of Hosea's call are uncertain and controverted. Did he suffer from the infidelity of a wife who left him for the allurement of life as a temple prostitute? Such would be the story if chapters 1 and 3 of the book of Hosea were descriptions of subsequent stages in their relationship. Or did Hosea simply marry a cult prostitute and place her in temporary seclusion as a sign of the purification needed prior to full relationship with Yahweh? In such a scenario the two chapters would represent two different accounts of the same event, with chapter 3 being autobiographical and chapter 1 written by a third party. The historical circumstances are complicated by the allusion to divorce (Hos 2:4) and the suggestion of a return to the honeymoon of desert life (vv. 16-19).

In any case, the tender affection of God is the basic truth and the alienating enticement experienced by Gomer became for Hosea a sign of the affection retained by Israel for the fertility cults of that age. The family bond established by the covenant was severely strained by the infidelity of Israel's affection for Baal. The fact that the Hebrew word *Baal* meant either "lord" or "husband" only enhanced the poetic imagery and religious irony of the case.

The children born to this strained symbolic marriage between Hosea and Gomer were given the chilling names of *Lo-ruhama* (literally, "she is not pitied"; 1:6) and *Lo-ammi* (literally, "not my people"; v. 8) to illustrate divine repudiation of Israel as announced by the life and message of Hosea. The decision is reversed when the names are changed to "Children of the Living God" and *Ruhama* "pitied" (3:1-3) as presumably the sign of a new beginning in Yahweh's relationship with his people. Hosea's reference to children illustrates his presumption that family bonds are created by covenant. Israel became a member of the divine family by adoption when the covenant was initiated. The imagery used by Hosea demonstrates the intimacy of that familial bond.

Hosea continues in that vein in what remains one of the most touching passages of the Hebrew Scriptures. Remembering the early affection of God for Israel, almost akin to that of a parent for a very young child, Hosea recalls that God taught Ephraim to walk, lifted the people in his arms and raised them to his cheek (11:1-9). The picture of a father, patiently guiding a youngster step by step into the first uncertain paces of a life-long journey, is a very powerful and endearing image (v. 3). For that reason, the Lord proclaimed through Hosea that he simply could not destroy his people in anger!

In the process of dealing with his unfaithful wife, Hosea spoke of Israel and invited a lawsuit against Israel, contending that "she is not my wife and I am not her husband" (Hos 2:4). This was the divorce formula of Israel. Later the prophet spoke in the name of the Lord, promising, "I will espouse you to me forever; I will espouse you in right (*sedeq*) and justice (*mishpat*), in love (*hesed*) and mercy (*rahamim*)" (v. 21).

For Hosea Israel was also like "the first fruits of a fig tree in its prime" (9:10) or a "luxuriant vine" (10:1) whose rich green foliage catches one's eye immediately. This type of imagery may seem less covenantal for it is more distant from the arena of human relationships, but it does imply a bond between field and farmer with life and death consequences for each. The care of a farmer for her choice garden also implies a deep and enduring bond. Isaiah also used agricultural imagery in the song of the vineyard (Is 5:1-7) to describe the care and attention lavished by God upon the chosen people.

On another occasion Jeremiah selected an image which accented the very intimate and personal nature of the relationship between Israel and the Lord, namely that of the fresh loincloth, first worn, then discarded and buried unwashed in the cleft of a rock. When retrieved, it was discovered to be "rotted and good for nothing" (Jer 13:1-11). The images are graphic and vivid. They should never be passed over quickly!

Each illustrates the bond in a new way. That relationship was covenantal through and through.

Readers of these prophetic texts often take for granted the familiar phrase "my people" since it occurs so often. It deserves more careful consideration because it expresses so succinctly the deep and abiding sense of divine possession and care. The way in which we use the personal possessive pronoun for our effects today may serve to illustrate the point. Anyone who speaks of "my car" presumes to use it at will, for whatever purpose may be convenient. The proud grandmother who insists on displaying the most recent snapshot of "my grandson" or the teenager who refers to "my sister" acknowledges a bond that endures through times of amiable chatter, genuine worry or bitter misunderstanding. Similarly, when a prophet addressed "my people" in the name of the Lord, the phrase asserted pride of possession, tender compassion and loyal support, but also some stern expectations at times. Only in this context does the lament of Micah, so familiar from the liturgy of Holy Week, "O my people, what have I done to you or how have I wearied you? Answer me!" (Mic 6:3) reveal its true poignancy.

The God of Jeremiah could say "I am a father to Israel; Ephraim is my first born" (Jer 31:9) and Jeremiah could purchase some land while the Babylonians were destroying the very walls of Jerusalem because he was supremely confident in the final victorious power of the covenant (32:1-44).

Faith

"Unless your faith is firm, you shall not be firm" (Is 7:9).

The expected human response to such a discerning choice on the part of God was faith. Behind all the specifics prescribed for ritual and life was the presumption that Israel would in fact obey. It remains a curious insight into the cultural psychology of Israel to observe that there is not a word for "obey" in Biblical Hebrew. The verb used consistently for this response is in fact *shama'*, "to hear"! Even a cursory reading of the prophets, especially those influenced by the theology of the Deuteronomist tradition reveals the repeated use of this word. Those who truly hear are presumed to obey, and to follow through in the actions of their lives as well as in the words of their lips.

When king Saul proudly if impetuously chose to save some of Amalek's flock for sacrifice, even though this had been expressly forbidden by the prophet Samuel, the prophet thundered his divinely inspired judgment that "obedience is better than sacrifice, and submission than the fat of rams!" (1 Sam 12:22). When Isaiah confronted King Ahaz who was busily preparing for siege in Jerusalem, the prophet demanded the only disposition deemed essential in God's eyes, namely faith (Is 7:9). Ahaz refused. Isaiah, who knew only too well the intrigues of the royal court and the commercial advantages of each military alliance, summarized as succinctly as anyone the basic command of the Lord: "For thus said the Lord God, the Holy One of Israel: By waiting and by calm you shall be saved, in quiet and trust your strength lies" (30:15).

This type of trust was rooted in the biblical notion and experience of the "Holy War" which was deemed holy because God was acknowledged as the primary warrior in the fray. Human beings contributed to the cause by believing that Yahweh and Yahweh alone was able to achieve final victory. Full trust and faith was the only response required of the Hebrews as they faced the Reed Sea with the Pharaoh's chariots in hot pursuit. "Fear not!" Moses commanded the people, "The Lord himself will fight for you; you have only to keep still" (Ex 14:13-14). Those who obeyed were saved because the Lord fought the battle in their behalf. Those without faith, however, had presumed to achieve victory by their own merits and strength, and were by that very fact assured of failure. In a similar fashion, Deuteronomy notes the obligation of the priests to encourage soldiers before battle, reminding them, "Be not weakhearted or afraid; be neither alarmed nor frightened, ... For it is the Lord your God who goes with you to fight for you against your enemies and give you victory" (Dt 20:3-4). Isaiah was a successor to that tradition and warned the king accordingly.

When Isaiah denounced those eager for constant military build-up in his day, he used words strangely reminiscent of issues which exercise the minds of modern critics. "Woe to those who depend on horses, who put their trust in chariots because of their number and in horsemen because of their combined power, but look not to the Holy One of Israel nor seek the Lord" (31:1). The voice of Israel's conscience attempted to call the royal cabinet back to the basics of faith. Isaiah spoke of the Lord's special election of Zion with great conviction and asked for nothing but faith. The philological root behind the term for faith is 'aman, meaning to "be firm, solid, or capable of sustaining pressure." Faith for Israel is something one can lean against with confidence, like a solid stone wall, as contrasted with a flimsy stage prop which might look strong but be most unstable. God was the only reality truly trustworthy for the prophets. Entrance into the covenant gave assurance of such stability and strength if embraced with true faith. Whether the instrument be Assyrian armies or modern nuclear weapons, the same negative assessment would come from the prophets, who encouraged dependence on God alone rather than upon mere human resources exclusively.

Jeremiah was also a prophet who struggled with the issue of military resistance, but the age had turned and a new reality was upon the stage of Israel's history. Jeremiah concluded that the power of Babylon in the seventh century B.C.E. was divinely blessed (Jer 34:2-7). Earlier in his life, Jeremiah had given a harsh critique of the Temple worship of his day. Before the King of Babylon had marshaled his military machinery against Jerusalem, Jeremiah had called for faith from those who replaced deeper personal commitment with mere ritual compliance and liturgical performance. "In speaking to your fathers on the day I brought them out of the land of Egypt, I gave them no command concerning holocaust or sacrifice," said Jeremiah; "This rather is what I commanded them: listen to my voice; then I will be your God and you will be my people" (7:22-23).

The final sentence in Jeremiah's oracle included the very words which were understood to establish a covenant as a binding reality for both parties. To speak the words was to create the bond, but it was conditioned by the human response of listening and obeying so rigorously demanded by the theology of the Deuteronomists. With an instinct deeply rooted in his relationship to the mystery of God, Jeremiah repeatedly called for true listening from everyone (11:4.7.10). When they refused, Jeremiah's God promised to share the same deafness in times of Israel's misfortunes (11:14). In the earlier judgment of Isaiah, the people preferred a covenant with death (Is 28:18) and this was finally brought to fulfillment when the battering rams of Babylon pounded against the city gates of Jerusalem, thus initiating a terrible time of looting, exile and death. The covenant refused by Israel marked the end of the era.

Those who did listen, however, showed themselves worthy of all the gifts and blessings inherent in the grace of the covenant. Israel had been chosen to become members of God's own family. Covenant always conferred the privilege of family bond, hence even Hosea could speak for the Lord, recalling "out of Egypt I called my son" (Hos 11:1). As a parent gives food and clothing to a child with lavish generosity, so would Isaiah be led to promise his neighbors in the Lord's name, "If you are willing and obey, you shall eat the good things of the land" (Is 1:19).

A Remnant In Their Midst

> "The remaining survivors of the house of Judah shall again strike root below and bear fruit above. For out of Jerusalem shall come a remnant, and from Mount Zion, survivors" (Is 37:31-32).

As centuries unfolded Israel experienced a growing realization of the way all nations were destined to share the blessings of the Lord's covenanted people. The call of Abraham included the promise that all nations would be blessed in him (Gen 12:3). Both Isaiah and Micah envisioned a day when all nations would stream toward the mountain of the Lord's house on Zion (Is 2:2-5; Mic 4:1-5). The last section of the book of Isaiah, probably written after the return of the exiles to Jerusalem from Babylon, even dreams of foreigners becoming servants in the temple which "shall be called a house of prayer for all peoples" (Is 56:7). In view of the demands of the covenant, however, a much smaller number remained among those faithful and loyal over the years.

Back in the time of Elijah, the prophet had fled from the wrath of Jezebel. On that journey he collapsed in exhaustion and despair under the broom tree on the way to Horeb. After being sustained by food offered by the Lord's messenger/angel, the prophet finally arrived at Horeb. His prayer at that holy site concluded with the observation that the Israelites had forsaken the Lord's covenant and killed his prophets. "I alone am left," he lamented, "and they seek to take my life" (1 K 19:9.14). The lone survivor experienced a sense of desolation as a result of fidelity to the Lord. Even though the text goes on to add that there were some seven thousand faithful persons left in Israel (v. 18), it was a small number in contrast to those who had moved to some practical allegiance to Baal.

Perhaps it was in that early age of persecution from Jezebel that the idea of a small number of chosen faithful entered the religious consciousness of Israel. The term used by the prophets was "remnant."

For us the image of remnant conjures up the idea of scraps of cloth remaining after a tailor has finished an article of clothing. Somehow remnants end up in the rag bag for patches or dust cloths if they are large enough. For Israel, however, it would seem that the term had its roots in the aftermath of military action.

Jeremiah, even though a later witness to the notion, provides a perfect illustration for its meaning. After Jerusalem had been destroyed by the Babylonians, only a few of the Judean leaders remained in the city. An earlier deportation in 597 B.C.E. had removed the cream of society and the military destruction had killed many during the final siege of the city in 587 B.C.E. They gathered around Jeremiah, begging his prayers "for all this remnant," once many in number and now only a few (Jer

42:2). They were the last survivors after the victorious enemy army had moved through the area, looting, pillaging and killing. It was a desperate group indeed, seeking protection and guidance from the prophet. They were the remnant (*sherit*).

The idea of remnant was not foreign to the traditions of Israel and Judah. The story of Noah, surviving by divine protection from the great flood (Gen 7:1ff), made him and his family the first "remnant" by the Lord's grace even if the word was not used as such. It was the prophet Isaiah who is most recognized for contributing the notion to the treasury of Israelite spirituality.

Isaiah repeatedly requested trust and confidence from Judah in the face of Assyrian invasion. The prophet invoked the covenantal loyalty and fidelity of the Lord for his people and assured the inhabitants of Jerusalem that they would be spared. When the city was in fact unharmed, its citizens and leaders erupted in jubilation, not thanksgiving, and Isaiah was profoundly disappointed (Is 22:1-14). His was a message which his people were somehow destined not to hear from the very beginning (6:9-10). Isaiah perceived that his neighbors were involved in an alliance of conspiracy (8:12) not the authentic covenant of Yahweh, and separated himself from them by divine command. He confided his instruction to a small circle of disciples (v. 16) and in this way provided a paradigm for Jesus of Nazareth after the rejection in Nazareth (Mk 6:1-13). Isaiah compared the faithful remnant to a tree trunk bereft of leaves (Is 6:13), which retains like the olive or willow the capacity for new sprouts and shoots.

His contemporary, Micah, also invoked the notion of remnant in those verses which date from the prophet himself as well as in later additions to the text. "I will assemble the remnant like a flock in the fold" said Micah (2:12). Later we read that God would assemble the outcasts and "make of the the lame a remnant, and of those driven far off a strong nation" (4:6-7). If the little ones who remain faithful represent the remnant in Israel, especially if they have survived a long and harsh war, perhaps the victims of domestic abuse and violence today fulfill the requirements and can count on all the blessings which the prophets promise to the faithful remnant!

The prophets insisted on the inevitability of divine protection and fidelity toward those who remained faithful to the covenant. It was an obligation assumed by Yahweh at the very inception of the covenant, "bestowing mercy (*ḥesed*) down to the thousandth generation, on the children of those who love me and keep my commandments" (Ex 20:6). That same covenantal fidelity supported each prophet in the crises of life. It was the result of the covenant that those who were faithful would experience opposition. Loyalty demanded hard choices sometimes and led to unpopular actions. Isaiah and his disciples seemed to stand alone in Jerusalem. So did Jeremiah and Baruch. It may seem like very small consolation indeed for Jeremiah to offer a promise of salvation in the larger context of the humiliation and destruction of Jerusalem, but his words to his disciple and scribe Baruch stand as the only hope given to the remnant: "Do you seek great things for yourself? Seek them not! I am bringing evil on all people, says the Lord, but your life I will leave you as booty, wherever you may go" (Jer 45:5).

The covenant was an invitation to all of Israel, and in some mysterious fashion, through Israel to all nations. Those who exercised zeal in behalf of the Lord, and thereby received his care and protection remained a small portion in the midst of the indifferent and hostile. That also remained a mystery. Since all things were somehow dependent upon the power of the Lord, Scripture spoke at times of the Lord "hardening hearts" (Ex 7:13.22) as a preparation for the grand revelation of salvation. The prophet often remained a surprisingly solitary figure in Israel, representing the entire nation in his struggle for faith and obedience.

※

Three questions which haunt the shadows of faith:

Why are some chosen for tough tasks in any given age?

Whence comes your assurance and confidence that God is with you?

Is the bond of covenant a vital factor in the lives of contemporary prophets?

4

Voices For The Poor

Our American culture prizes individualism and presumes personal independence. By contrast the world of the Hebrew prophets emphasized the social bonds which were concretely enfleshed in each person. They assumed a community aspect for everything. Some insight may come from modern Japanese culture which stresses the team spirit in each venture.

The people of Israel were chosen by God for a purpose. The "call from" was inevitably experienced as a "call to." Their prophets were called from the covenanted community in order to be symbols of the vocation which was shared by all. Almost by definition the prophet exercised a ministry of social responsibility, calling everyone's attention to the bond of unity which characterized Yahweh's people. Bonded together, they bore responsibility for meeting each others' needs.

Precisely when the Hebrews were enslaved in Egypt and forced to bear the burdens of difficult manual labor under unjust conditions (Ex 3:7-8; 5:6-18), Yahweh had intervened to free them from oppression. Such was their beginning; consequently Yahweh was forever the One who "brought them out of the land of Egypt, out of the house of slaves" as the opening words of the Decalogue declared (20:1). Yahweh was the God who listened to the cry of the oppressed, just as he had when the Hebrews were tearfully building the Pharaoh's storehouses (3:7f).

The Cry Of The Poor

"The Lord looked for judgment (*mishpat*), but see, bloodshed (*mispah*)! For justice (*sedeqah*), but hark, the outcry (*sa'aqah*)!" (Is 5:7).

The cry which Yahweh heard was not the generic lament of the sad and bereaved, nor the familiar sobbing of punished or disappointed children. Rather, this cry (*sa'aqah* as found in both Is 5:7 and the account of the slavery in Egypt in Ex 3:7) was the technical term for the legal action of a plaintiff seeking justice from legitimate authority (see Ex 22:23). It described a law suit in Israel's courts. Yahweh's direct and personal response to the cry of the Hebrew people was a never forgotten action which initiated the Exodus.

The prophets had sharp ears in God's name. They listened to the news of the day with senses attuned to the special frequency reserved for the poor, almost like a special channel on the prophetic CB radio of the day.

In fact the term Hebrew itself (*'Apiru/Habiru*) originally referred to a social class of marginalized workers, less affluent than their more established neighbors and probably dependent on others at times for survival even though they had a reputation for toughness. Only later did the term become something of an ethnic or quasi-national description. Just as this people was politically and economically disenfranchised by original definition; so also their Yahweh was originally revered as One who defended the oppressed and liberated those in need. Recent theories regarding the historical events of the Exodus include the assimilation of oppressed Canaanite slaves in rebellion as well as the victorious conquest of the land by Joshua and his armies from the Egyptian wilderness.

This deity required that his people be ever active in

similarly reaching out to those in need in successive generations. The Code of the Covenant (Ex 21:1—23:23), a
collection of basic obligations for the recently freed and newly
settled Hebrews, stipulated freedom for all Hebrew slaves after
six years of work (20:2). The same Code also clearly placed
human relationships as religious duties more significant than
ritual performance (vv. 7-32). Continued fidelity to that
tradition requires a similar sense of priority in our day as well.
The Gospel of Matthew quotes Jesus who insisted on the
prophet Hosea's conviction that covenantal loyalty and mercy
is more important than sacrifice (Mt 9:13; 12:7). The obligation
of Hebrews not to take advantage of strangers or exploit them
was consistently motivated by the recollection that they
themselves had been in similar straits in Egypt (Ex 22:21);
therefore Yahweh promised to hear the cry of any widow or
orphan oppressed by a member of the Hebrew nation (v. 22).
The poor had a special claim on Yahweh. Initially they had
become his people in Egypt when they called for his assistance.
In later ages during the days of the judges, Yahweh repeatedly
responded in times of duress, even when the difficulty was of
their own doing (Jgs 3:9.15; 4:3 etc.). All this provides background for the first beatitude in Luke's account of the Sermon
of the Mount, "Blessed are you poor, the Kingdom of God is
yours!" (Lk 6:20).

Early Prophetic Interventions

"In the place where the dogs licked up the blood of Naboth, the
dogs shall lick up your blood too" (1 K 21:19).

Zeal for the God of the covenant moved the earliest known
prophets to side with those whose rights were being ignored.
When David violated the marriage bond between the loyal
and upright Uriah the Hittite and his wife Bathsheba, the

prophet Nathan slyly proposed the parable of the man with his one prized ewe lamb and elicited a self-condemnation from the lips of David (2 Sam 12:1-14). Nathan then denounced David for his blatant disrespect for the rights of the less powerful members of his people.

Some hundred and fifty years later Elijah confronted King Ahab for the illegal methods used by his wife Jezebel to obtain the much coveted vineyard of poor Naboth in violation of covenant command and common decency. By obtaining false witnesses who would swear against Naboth, he could be executed and his land annexed to the royal estates (1 K 21:1-24). As a result Elijah's voice rises forever against the powerful who abuse legal means to cheat the defenseless of their property. The text cited above represents the punishment proclaimed against King Ahab for countenancing the spilling of Naboth's innocent blood for the sake of personal comfort and greedy gain.

Elisha intervened to save a widow from her creditors by miraculously multiplying her store of oil so that she could sell her sudden surplus and thus save her sons from indentured slavery (2 K 4:1-7). On another occasion Gehazi, the servant of Elisha, interceded with the king to obtain the restoration of the property lost by another widow during the famine (8:1-6).

Thus from the very beginning Israel's prophets were remembered as persons actively securing the rights of the poor in the face of royal authority or wealthy lenders who would deny those rights. Yahweh cared for the poor and so did those called to be his special servants. Anyone claiming the title or task of God's prophet must be wide-eyed and attentive to the needs of the poor. Conversely, even the most zealous and scrupulous servant of Yahweh who neglects the just cause of the needy is dismissed as spurious and self-serving by the biblical witness. In the eyes of the Bible, no one who does not care for the poor (Mic 7:2) can be acclaimed a saint (usually termed *hasid* in Hebrew which literally refers to one who is faithful to obligations of mutual care for the well-being of God and neighbor).

Economic Development (For Some)

> "Woe to you who join house to house, who connect field with field, till no room remains, and you are left to dwell alone in the midst of the land" (Is 5:8).

It is against this backdrop that we learn of the economic development which occurred in northern Israel during the eighth century B.C.E. According to the major archaeological excavations, earlier levels of inhabitation reveal a remarkable similarity in the homes occupied by the people who first moved into Canaan during the thirteenth century B.C.E. Single-level homes with three simple rooms facing an open-air courtyard were the standard models of the age. They are generally called "four room houses." Portions of the roofs were strengthened to support some storage, drying of food and even some gathering of the family in the cool of the evening. Cooking and a variety of domestic industries were done in the courtyard. The walls provided corners for ovens, grain silos and work areas for weaving or pottery making.[1]

---

[1] Philip J. King work, entitled *Amos, Hosea, Micah: An Archaeological Commentary* (Westminster, 1988) presents the archaeological background for many of the references found in the eighth century B.C.E. prophets with ample illustrations. Readers should be alerted to studies in biblical sociology and anthropology which highlight the differing significance of social institutions of biblical times from the same human realities of our post industrial age. As an example I would recommend B. Malina, *The New Testament World: Insights from Cultural Anthropology* (John Knox Press, 1981).

During the eighth century B.C.E., however, we notice a sharp distinction between the homes of the rich and the poor in places like Tirzah, the capital of the northern kingdom for several generations (1 K 15:33; 16:6.8.15.17.23), or Shechem, the traditional site for covenant renewal and the shrine where Rehoboam went to be acclaimed king after the death of Solomon (Jos 24:1; 1 K 12:1). Larger and more sturdy stone homes with second stories for more gracious living and cedar decoration began to gravitate toward the western edges of the city mounds. Thus the prevailing strong western breezes cooled those houses in hot weather, even blowing dust or unpleasant smells eastward toward the poorer sections of the city. At Tirzah a wall actually separated the well-built houses from their less affluent neighbors. Such "slums" were undoubtedly the occasion for strong prophetic reaction to this violation of covenantal unity. The *hesed*, that is, the mutual covenantal fidelity, of Yahweh's people had been seriously violated.

Contemporary urban slums almost seem a given in our age, and in most large cities the stark contrast is hidden by larger city areas and vaster numbers of inhabitants. On both counts Hebrew towns were very small by comparison. The prophets of Israel or Judah however would not allow themselves to be so easily distracted from the bitter reality of the contrast between the rich and poorer members of the covenanted family. The Dow Jones was up, but only for some, and the prophets noted it clearly.

Justice And Righteousness

"If you would offer me holocausts, then let justice (*mishpat*) surge like water and goodness (*sedeqaḥ*) like an unfailing stream" (Am 5:23-24).

One of the fundamental categories used by Hebrew culture to judge the rightness of things is that of "justice." Much more than a legal concept, it extended over wide and diverse areas of life. The basic Semitic root *sdq* seems to mean "to be firm, strong, straight, or right." In that sense any object has a share of justice when it is somehow appropriate to its nature, faithful to its inner purpose, and in harmony with its function. An object or person is just when it is properly related. To be just is to be correct, not in isolated splendor, but in relation to others, their needs and purposes.

A path for example, is just when it leads where it should with directness and ease (Ps 23:3). A weight or measure is just when it actually corresponds to the label it bears (Am 8:5; Ez 45:10) and a sacrifice is just when it is properly offered according to the requirements of the donor, agent or divine recipient (Ps 4:6). God is just when he demonstrates his own divine standards and acts accordingly. Human judges are just when they act according to the true nature of things, not becoming shortsighted by reason of mere external circumstances or bribes (Is 11:3-4). For the prophets as for all Hebrews, divine propriety is justice, for Yahweh upholds the rightness of all his creatures at their deepest level.

The noun *sedeqah* is often translated "righteousness" in the more common biblical versions. This may be unfortunate because the English usage of the term seems to smack of superiority and a certain self-serving distance from others not so upright or moral. The deeper meaning of the term, however, suggests interdependence and profound respect for the needs of others. Such is justice in the minds and on the lips of the Hebrew prophets. The more genuine Hebrew notion is reflected in the practice of labeling the metal poorboxes affixed to the Western Wall of the ancient Temple (also called the

Wailing Wall by some) with the simple term *"sedeqah"*! The custom catches tourists and observant pilgrims by surpise. To suggest that alms containers might be intended for the regular restoration of justice in our world leaves the observant pilgrims with much to ponder.

The other Hebrew term frequently encountererd in this connection is *mishpat.* Its basic stem is the verb *shpt* which means "to set something up, to judge, to act decisively, to exercise leadership, to intervene and bring a human situation to an appropriate resolution." *Mishpat* is the noun which describes the resulting decision or action. Such actions tend to create precedents. They can become customary procedures or repeated practices in subsequent generations. For that reason the noun brings with it a certain sense of the insititutionalized way of dealing with things. It suggests social structures which support and enhance human relationships. It is often translated "justice" but means ways of doing things. When Moses introduces the Decalogue in the book of Deuteronomy, he describes them as "statutes and decrees (*mishpatim*)" (Dt 5:1).

Although the terms *sedeqah* and *mishpat* are often used in what might seem to be an interchangeable fashion, they each bear slightly different nuances. Together they stress the rightness and expected functioning of the topic under scrutiny. The citation from Amos at the beginning of this section suggests that true worship results in a combination of justice and judgment similar to refreshing and life-giving torrents of cold water for thirsty people.

American society is very familiar with the concept of "rights." They are guaranteed by the Constitution and fiercely protected by civil law even if tragic violations of racial dignity or other freedoms have in fact marred our national history at times. Our fundamental American perspective is to view such rights as things owed to us as individuals and citizens. The biblical notion of "rights" inherent in justice is rather the duties and obligations which one member of the covenant has toward others. In its daily practice it was more other-directed than self-concerned. The difference may be subtle, but it also helps explain the fact that alms could bear the label "justice (*sedeqah*)."

Amos—A Person Consumed By Justice

"Yes, I know how many are your crimes, how grievous your sins: oppressing the just, accepting bribes, repelling the needy at the gate!" (Am 5:12).

It was sometime near 750 B.C.E. when Amos a shepherd and dresser of sycamores from Tekoa strode into Bethel, the ancient shrine and royal sanctuary of the northern kingdom of Israel. His home town was situated in the rugged and rocky area south of Jerusalem. The harshness of that region may have contributed to the starkness of the prophet's judgments. In a land where mountains and rocks cast shadows rather than trees or shrubs, and where the only natural beauty was the blue sky and the rosy hue of the scattered stones at sunset, it was easy to absorb the clarity of the landscape and to see all things in terms of life and death, black and white. From the ruins of Tekoa one can almost look down on the tops of the mountains as they fall away toward the Jordan valley to the east. Even today one can easily sing songs from that vantage point about Yahweh who "strides upon the heights of the earth" (Am 4:13). Amos was not a professional prophet by background; at least that seems to be the sense of his response to the sneering priest Amaziah at Bethel (7:14), but rather one whose personal insight into the plight of the poor forced him to speak in the name of Yahweh.

Read the entire book of Amos to experience the chilling power of his words. Keep in mind our own society with all its enticing advertising on television to promote the "good life." How many of our urban or rural poor can experience such a life style? What types of values are being promoted? How much injustice undergirds it all?

Amos undoubtedly listed the major covenantal crimes of Israel (2:6-8) as he stood in the courtyard of the shrine at Bethel, but the shocking center of his speech, at least as it was summarized and reported by Amaziah, was the traitorous prophetic announcement of the death of King Jeroboam II and the exile of the northern tribes (7:11)! When the priest Amaziah attempted to dismiss him and send him back to his own land of Judah, Amos responded with vigor, explicitly including the priest's own wife and children in the disaster he already sensed (v. 17). Such is the price paid by all who are accomplices to those who would silence the prophet's voice.

The world into which Amos came was prosperous. The markets and gates teemed with merchants from the coastal cities of Phoenicia. Although King Omri was given short shrift and a decidedly negative review in biblical chronicles (1 K 16:23-26), he truly established political stability and prosperity in the northern kingdom. Ahab and Jezebel had continued that effort during the days of Elisha. Although the dynasty had been overthrown by General Jehu in the name of Yahweh and with prophetic blessing, the affluence of the cities continued. By the time of Jeroboam II in the mid-eighth century B.C.E., a veneer of truly gracious charm was found in the lives of leaders in each city.

Reading through the book of Amos as it exists today, one can see small hints of the elegance which marked the lives of the more wealthy citizens of Bethel and neighboring towns.

Some possessed winter and summer homes, with decorations sufficiently ostentatious as to allow Amos the chance to describe them sarcastically as "apartments of ivory" (Am 3:15). Blissfully ignorant or indifferent to the oppression of the poor outside their homes, the matrons simply signaled for a drink, never knowing that in the eyes of Amos they were nothing but "fat cows of Bashan" (4:1). Their lives were filled with ease and comfort (6:1). Amos paints their picture with his words, portraying them stretched out on beds of ivory, feasting on tender stall-fed veal, against elegant musical background, sipping wine from imported bowls and anointing themselves with the finest oils and lotions (vv. 4-6).

Behind this facade of luxury Amos saw an impatient eagerness for dishonest profit and a deliberate shortening of weights to amass the fortune needed to sustain that type of "good life" (8:5). His allusions to affluence, almost like advertisements in modern magazines, were not very positively presented. Amos saw the homes and palaces filled with violence and robbery, not items of art (3:10). He saw the quick wink or knowing nod which signaled the bribes exchanged at the city gate where justice was supposed to be distributed to all the children of Israel (5:12). He saw the banquets of the rich as if those gathered were in fact swallowing the very lives of the poor and needy (8:4).

With bitterness Amos denounced those who would sell the poor and needy for a pair of shoes (2:6 and 8:6). Perhaps the allusion is to the sordid ease with which lives were given such a cheap price in the open markets of palace negotiations. Another possibility is that Amos was in fact alluding to the mysterious ritual custom, whose origin is probably buried in ancient practices by which obligation could be legally terminated by loosening a shoe and spitting (Dt 25:9). If the latter is intended, the phrase is a denunciation of actions, in fact ethically and socially immoral, but protected by external legality. In every age a loophole can be found by those determined to exploit others for their own gain. Nursing homes that follow the letter of the law, but ignore the needs of their patients, realtors who impose impossible monthly payments in order to foreclose at a later time, or husbands who take advantage of existing laws to defraud divorced spouses of needed child support all fit into this latter interpretation of Amos' category of the "shoe business" today.

Under the facade of elegant living Amos sensed a desperate greed. Amos described the desire for land as so intense that the wealthy of Israel "panted after the very dust on the heads of the poor" (2:7 in the Jerusalem Bible)! This translation represents a graphic alternative to the New American Bible's version of the verse, namely "They trample the heads of the weak into the dust of the earth." Such vivid imagery remains for a long time after any thoughtful reading of the sermons preached by Amos to the populace gathered at Bethel for worship.

Amos was consumed by the injustice of the society in which he lived. He saw, not the sweet wine of the cool, shaded marketplaces, but the bitter lives of those who produced it. He studied, not the firm clean stone buildings just inside the city gates, but the harsh attitudes of their inhabitants toward the less fortunate across the city. He saw an entire social structure built upon injustice and exploitation. The repeated violation of covenantal bonds was a glaring truth which Amos could not avoid. He begged for justice in actions and truly respectful customs which would flow through the uneven city streets like running water fresh from the skies, purifying everything (5:24).

Translated into a modern scene, Amos would look through smart office windows to see the desperate lives of those who clean them each night. He would see beyond the fresh attractive displays of fruit and vegetables in our supermarkets to the bent backs of Central America where entire families move slowly through each field in the hot sun, harvesting the fields at very meager wages to bring fresh melons and tomatoes to our tables when out of season in more northern climates. Amos served a God who had delivered the poor and afflicted from Egypt, a God who hears the cry of all who suffer in similar straits of any age. Amos would always wonder about the conditions in the factory which produced our inexpensive bargain gadgets somewhere in the Far East. It was a consuming preoccupation for him. Once we allow ourselves to see the world's injustice through Amos' eyes of faith, it never looks quite as pretty again.

Micah-An Echo From The South

"The women of my people you drive from their pleasant houses; from their children, you take away forever the honor I gave them" (Mic 2:9).

Amos was not alone. Similar outcries rose from other parts of the land. To the south, Micah of Moresheth (probably a small Judean village west of Jerusalem) witnessed the unacceptable appropriation of the property of widows by more powerful families and the eager accumulation of the fields by new land owners (Mic 2:1.9). This was particularly offensive to him because he was dedicated to the traditional Hebrew respect for family inheritances. Micah knew that they were sacred gifts from Yahweh and he recognized the duty of passing that treasure from one generation to the next. Like

Elijah before him, Micah respected the dignity of the powerless and their enduring responsibility to care for the land of their ancestors. He did not tolerate the practice of those who took over the land of the needy in his day, and would be equally harsh with those who casually dispossess the troubled farmer today in order to obtain an additional tax break in the form of holdings. His caustic attack on the leaders compared them to cannibals, greedily eating the flesh of their own people and making stew of the poor (3:1-3). Profit as primary motive and dismissal of the obligation to care for others united in the bonds of covenant was unacceptable to Micah in any age. The inevitable result of such activities in Micah in any age. The inevitable result of such activities in Michah's prophetic eyes was the destruction of Samaria, the captial of the Northern Kingdom, and the reduction of Jerusalem to a rubble heap of stones in the field (1:6; 3:12).

Read the first three chapters of the book of Micah and hear the strident tones of his warnings and judgments.

Isaiah—The Gentleman From Jerusalem

"Woe to the champions at drinking wine, the valiant at mixing strong drink! To those who acquit the guilty for bribes, and deprive the just man of his rights!" (Is 5:22-23).

As a citizen of virtually the same decades, Isaiah saw similarly grim pictures of injustice from the streets of Jerusalem. With what seems to have been easy access to royal circles, Isaiah was able to frequent the homes of the leaders of the city. He was brutal in his mimicry of the wealthy women he saw on the streets (3:18-23). His fundamental prophetic experiences of personal and collective guilt cleansed by Yahweh (6:5-7) led him to insist on confidence in Yahweh rather than in all the various forms of material security which people accumulated. The words cited above sound uncannily like a complaint about modern suburban cocktail parties where boasting about business deals follows a few rounds of drinks! Because Isaiah was so convinced of the need and duty to trust Yahweh above all (30:15), he denounced the wealth garnered at the expense of the poor. Thus the starting point of Isaiah may have been different from that of Amos, but the conclusion was similar and equally sharp.

Read Isaiah 1-12 and 28-32 for the full flavor of this remarkable poet and critic of life in Jerusalem.

Speaking in the name of Yahweh as prophets were called to do, Isaiah examined the hands of those gathered in prayer, and rejected them as "filled with blood" (1:15). With his own brand of satire Isaiah described the princes of the city as "loving bribes and running after gifts," refusing to defend orphans or to hear the legal petitions of widows (1:23). In another text the same leaders are condemned for devouring vineyards and keeping the spoil of the poor in their houses (3:14), almost as if it were a war trophy or a collectible objet d'art. Real estate acquisition must have been as much of a moral issue in Jerusalem as in Moresheth, for Isaiah echoed Micah by pronouncing "Woe to those who join house to house, adding field to field until there is no more room and you are made to dwell alone in the land" (5:8). He detested those who were heroes at the drinking bowl, full of bravado in a moment of revelry with friends, but so cowardly as to acquit the guilty for a bribe and deprive the innocent of justice. Crimes reported in the newspapers, especially those which escape punishment because of personal friendship with civic leaders, would be clearly seen by Isaiah for the crimes they were.

In a society of tight family bonds, and indeed with emphasis upon a person's relationship to the patriarchal figure of responsibility, those most abandoned were precisely widows and orphans. Without resources for sustenance, they were reduced to slavery, begging or prostitution for survival. For that reason widows and orphans became the familar symbol of people in desperate need. Much earlier Ugaritic society had also recognized the desperate plight of these people and judged kings according to their willingness to feed widows and orphans from their table. The Code of the Covenant singled them out as worthy of help always (Ex 22:21-23), and the humanitarian concern of Deuteronomy selected them as privileged recipients of aid in time of festival celebration (Dt 16:11). Isaiah may have been influenced by Deuteronomic theologians fleeing to Jerusalem and sanctuary under Hezekiah at the time of the Assyrian destruction of Samaria (722 B.C.E.), or he may simply have been very traditional in regularly listing them as examples of need in the city of his age. In a similar fashion, we mention a familiar modern litany of groups such as "street people, elderly and abused women or children" when drawing the attention of our age to people in desperate need without the protection of the larger society within which they are forced to live.

Dreams Of The King Yet To Come

"He shall judge the poor with justice, and decide aright for the land's afflicted" (Is 11:4).

Each time a new successor of David assumed royal responsibility in Judah, the people garnered once again all the ancient hopes for a ruler worthy of the task. They remembered the best of David and they summoned prophets like Isaiah to utter oracles in the name of Yahweh. Such words blessed the new king and promised a fresh a start for all. The oracles in poetic form are called messianic because they are addressed to the anointed one (*meshiah*). They gradually became associated with the dreams of Israel and Judah for that final future age when Yahweh's salvation would be definitively experienced in this world. What began as messianic in the sense of royal became messianic in the sense of final and future. The dreams started with new kings. Prophets were around each time to remind court and lowly citizen of the true task of the person being enthroned.

In the two messianic hymns of Isaiah an urgent hope for justice was clearly highlighted. One sung rhapsodically of peace without end and "justice (*mishpat*) and righteousness (*sedeqah*) from this time forth and forever" (9:7). The other proclaimed that the new king, probably Hezekiah, would see beyond mere externals, "judging the poor with rightness (*sedeqah*), and deciding with equity for the meek of the earth" (11:4).

Although the original focus for these hymns may have been Hezekiah, son and successor to the despised Ahaz, the words of Isaiah took on life of their own and were applied to various successive rulers, and finally to the one long desired royal Deliverer. In even later centuries the first Christian communities saw the great care of Jesus for the poor as an expression and fulfillment of Isaiah's prophetic dream. Throughout all that time each generation held its leaders responsible for maintaining the rightness of things and demanded that as leaders within the covenanted community they show special respect for those unable to obtain justice by their own power.

The messianic hymns of Isaiah have become a litmus test

for every person called to leadership. The voiceless and powerless need to be restored to harmony with the larger community.
Their gifts call for respect and development in service to all.
The practices of every group, be it a neighborhood gathering of
mutual support for the elderly, a workers' union or the
organizational committees of a corporate board of directors,
should sustain and promote the good of all, especially the
weakest members. That's the way Isaiah saw things.

Jeremiah—A Final Call

> "They go their wicked way; justice they do not defend by
> advancing the claim of the fatherless or judging the cause of the
> poor. Shall I not punish these things says the Lord?"
> (Jer 5:28-29)

century later the larger political horizon had changed as
lon succeeded Assyria in world power and leadership.
Unfortunately, the perverse pettiness of local princes and
priests had not changed. The prophet Zephaniah denounced
the leaders of Jerusalem for their houses filled with "violence
and deceit" (Zeph 1:9). He saw the imminent destruction of
Jerusalem and invited the poor to seek Yahweh (2:3). He
reminded them that Yahweh was truly in their midst, "bringing
his justice (*mishpat*) to light each morning" (3:5). With that
imagery and reference to the morning sunshine, Zephaniah
stood in solidarity with ancient Mesopotamian religions which
saw the sun (*shemesh* in Hebrew) as a symbol for Shamshu, the
god of justice. He also stood united to later Christians who
welcomed Jesus, the Sun of Justice, as the Dawn of salvation
by which all things would be restored to their original rightness
(Lk 1:78). Nothing stays hidden in the shadows.

Better known as a representative of that age is Jeremiah

whose inner struggles with the message he carried are so well documented. Although dating from the end of the seventh century B.C.E., the words of Jeremiah provide consolation for all who are compelled to say hard things to those they love and serve.

Like his predecessors Jeremiah complains about those who refuse to judge the causes of orphans justly (Jer 5:28). He peers into the great temple at Jerusalem and denounces it as a "den of robbers" (7:11) because those who frequent its festivals are unconcerned about justice toward aliens, widows and orphans (v. 6). He walks the streets of Jerusalem looking in vain for one truly honest person (5:1), but sees sadly that "all, from the least to the greatest, are greedy for unjust gain" (8:10). For Jeremiah the root cause of injustice is not so much the refusal to trust in Yahweh as described by Isaiah, but rather the pervasive dishonesty and deceitfulness which infects everyone with its sickness and disease (9:3-6). For Jeremiah Yahweh remains someone who "practices covenantal love (*hesed*), justice (*mishpat*) and rightness (*sedeqah*) on earth" (9:23). This verse is a remarkable summary of the Lord's work and the ethical mandate given to those who would profess faith in that same Lord.

In his concern for justice, Jeremiah reserves his major volley for King Jehoiakim, son of the saintly King Josiah. In contrast to his father, Jehoiakim expanded his palace without rightness (*sedeq*) and his terraces without justice (*mishpat*), refusing just wages to those who labored to build his spacious upper rooms, well-windowed to catch the evening breezes, paneled in cedar and even painted in vermillion (22:13-17).

Those words still cut deeply and sting, even after twenty-five centuries! They cut clergy who build splendid residences at the expense of the pressing family needs of neighboring folk,

as well as doctors whose suburban dwellings are paid for by
Medicare fraud. They excoriate those who would build pre-
tentious public structures through revenue raised by sales
taxes on food or other items necessary for the day to day
existence of the poor. Jeremiah does not burn with the precise
type of anger reflected in Amos; He knows his own pain and
weak humanity too well. Nevertheless, he does denounce the
corrosive dishonesty of those who exploit others by proposing
motives which were in fact untrue and unfounded in order to
serve their own purposes.

Other prophets followed in similar vein. Habakkuk, another
contemporary of Jeremiah, laments towns built with blood
(Hab 2:12). Ezekiel is preoccupied with his own vision of
Yahweh's glory departing in utter disdain from the ritually
polluted temple. Nevertheless, Ezekiel refuses to see correct
ritual as the sole measurement of decency and moral fiber. In
his famous text regarding individual responsibility, Ezekiel
contrasts three generations of good and evil persons. In each
case robbery, oppression of the poor and lending at interest
join pagan ritual as signs of truly unacceptable moral behavior
(Ez 18:5-9.10-13.14-18). They are words worthy of any
contemporary examination of conscience and could well be
written over the doors of highrise corporate offices and modern
simple bungalows as well. For rich and poor alike they list the
areas which drive divine glory from our midst. Justice remains
somehow central.

What does one say about the stinging denunciation of
injustice found in virtually every pre-exilic prophet of Israel?
Do we dismiss them as a particular problem of another age?
Do we accept the statements as expressions of overly tender
consciences? Or do we conclude that Yahweh, the God of the
Hebrew covenant and the Father of Jesus, has very rigorous

demands which will not be silenced? To hear these words, especially in communal worship, is to sense the divine call to reexamine the social fabric of every human venture. These prophetic words force us to wonder about the conditions which exist wherever anything is produced for human consumption. The facile transportation of our modern world and the current global markets may render existing injustice less visible, but not less culpable, or so say the prophets of Israel. They speak to people of affluence and power everywhere. They speak to people without power, but consumed with greed nonetheless. The prophets would not allow a person raiding garbage cans for food on the very day of Lady Liberty's American rededication in 1986 to go unnoticed. Nor would they politely ignore the so-called "red lining" of certain residential areas destined for decline and quick profit when loans are not readily available. The 1986 pastoral letter of the American bishops continues to ask some of the questions first posed by Hebrew prophets who loved Yahweh's poor enough to raise the harder questions of life.

※

Three voices in behalf today's poor:

Who are the people exploited by the prosperity experienced in your life?

Who speaks in their behalf today?

How is the Lord intervening in their favor?

5

Sacrifices And Festivals

Like people of all ages, Israel loved festivals. There was moreover a special type of spontaneity which marked the lives of Near Eastern nations along the Mediterrean shore; their religious assemblies became opportunities for expressing that cultural characteristic. They possessed a dynamic understanding of human nature and presumed that all human thoughts would inevitably flow into action. Just as they forbade covetous thoughts and desires (Ex 20:17), they likewise stipulated community festivals of faith. Theirs was a natural wholistic concept of life. Faith had to be expressed in some external fashion.

Speaking in behalf of his restless people in Egypt, Moses and Aaron had confronted the Pharaoh and demanded, with the Lord's demand, "Let my people go, that they may celebrate a feast (literally serve) to me in the desert" (Ex 5:1). As the text records it, freedom of religious expression was at the root of the Exodus experience. The Hebrew word often used for what we would term liturgy was 'abadah, literally translated as "service" or "slavery." The word is related to the term 'ebed which is "servant/slave.". The use of the term servant in the daily speech of the Hebrews was a self-depreciating reference which often found expression in a liturgical context of worship of the Great Lord before whom all human beings are very humble subordinates. The psalms as songs of Temple worship are filled with references to this word. Our own English usage of the phrase "the time of services" at the local parish stems from the same origin and perspective. Obviously, the word stands perennially as judge of the reality.

After the powerful experience on Sinai (described in increasingly liturgical terms as evidenced in the sign promised to Moses in Ex 3:12) and Israel's entrance into the land of Canaan, three major festivals punctuated each year. The Hebrew word used for such celebrations was *hag*, which is usually translated "pilgrimage festival." The Hebrew root itself is *hagag* which means "to dance, to be festive" and suggests the type of celebrations included in each pilgrimage. The word is also related to the name of the post-exilic prophet Haggai (whose name actually means "festive," an appropriate label for one who encouraged the rebuilding and rededication of the Temple in Jerusalem after the Exile).

The so-called Code of the Covenant specifies these three as the Feast of the Unleavened Bread (also called Passover though these may have been two separate celebrations which later merged by reason of being celebrated at the same time of the year), the first Grain Harvest (called Pentecost since it was celebrated fifty days later), and Tabernacles or Booths as the final celebration at the end of the Autumn harvest (23:14-17; see also Dt 16:1-17). On these three occasions each year all adult males were required to gather for a communal celebration of gratitude for blessings received. They did not come empty-handed, but rather came with gifts for sacrifice and with families to share in the festivities. At first they gathered at the local shrines and high places. Later under the centralizing nudge of Deuteronomy, Jerusalem itself became the focus of their travels and pilgrimage.

There has been some question regarding the existence of an annual Enthronement festival in Jerusalem, somewhat parallel to the rituals of Mesopotamia. Psalms such as 93 and 97-99 declare that the Lord is King. They also contain many references to ritual as well as the clear acknowledgment of the sovereignty of Yahweh in Zion. This element may have been a facet of the celebration of Tabernacles. Prophets certainly lived in awe of the Lord, even if such a Feast did not exist on a regular basis.[1]

Worship and Pilgrimage

"For seven days you shall celebrate this pilgrim feast in honor of the Lord, your God, in the place which he chooses; since the Lord, your God, has blessed you in all your crops and in all your undertakings" (Dt 16:15).

The timing of these festivals indicates rather clearly that they were woven into the annual agricultural cycle of the villages. At the appropriate time the people gathered to acknowledge joyously the multiple gifts of the Lord as reflected in the presence of new leaven or in the move to Spring pastures which occurred at roughly the same month.[2] The people also celebrated the major harvests of the year. Coming from small villages or nomadic settlements scattered across the countryside, they converged on the shrines to express in ritual

---

[1]S. Mowinckel, *The Psalms in Israel's Worship* (Blackwell, 1962) I, 106-192.

[2]R. de Vaux, *Studies in Old Testament Sacrifice* (University of Wales, 1964) 1-26.

gesture and song their faith-filled gratitude for all the material blessings received.

For those of us who live surrounded by plentiful supplies of food, it is difficult to imagine life totally dependent upon the harvest each year. Without preservation by such modern discoveries as canning or freezing, food could only be spiced or dried if it was to be preserved. It wasn't long after the harvest each year that rationing came into daily usage in virtually every household. Bread was baked each morning and flour carefully measured out for the day. Left-overs were unheard of and the supplies became very thin as the months went by. The time of the new harvest was indeed something to celebrate, and they did, for their thoughts always overflowed into action.

For later generations the Deuteronomic tradition spelled out very clearly the obligations of pilgrimage festivals and the spirit which should pervade those celebrations. Concerned with the elimination of the Canaanized highplaces and the centralization of true worship in the Temple of Jerusalem, the theology of Deuteronomy spelled out the fact that the Name of the Lord dwelled in the Temple, even though no mere human building could contain the full majesty of God's presence. The prayer of Solomon, uttered on the occasion of the formal dedication of that same Temple, spelled out the theology in a profoundly engaging fashion (1 K 8:27-30). Legislation included in the book of Deuteronomy, particularly for the great festival of Tabernacles, stipulated the spirit of joy and faith which should mark the week-long celebration each year (Dt 16:15).

On such occasions the people of God came into being once more. The entire nation, like the actions of their feast, became visible as a people united in faith. They were audible as well, in their songs and excited chatter. The festival enabled all to see and experience their common allegiance to Yahweh the God of the covenant, and therefore their mutual bond with each other.

In the earliest years it was the feast of Tabernacles or Booths which served as the major festival each year. During the weeks of harvest people lived in rough, thatched shelters out in the fields to protect them from marauders. Afterwards they brought a portion of the produce to the local highplace, or in later centuries, to the Temple in Jerusalem. There they entered into the ritual celebration of the renewal of the covenant (Dt 26:1-11). Since the biblical text does not provide any one single description of the precise ritual used on the Feast of Tabernacles, its elements must be gleaned from a scattering of citations.[3] The exercise entailed in sifting the Scriptures for references to the events surrounding the pilgrimage festivals is necessary to appreciate the background for the strong prophetic statements in these festivals.

Runners from the neighboring sanctuary would pass through each village announcing the feast according to the careful calculations of the lunar calendar. Some of the psalms seem to contain references to the official invitation as reflected in words such as "I rejoiced because they said to me, 'we will go up to the house of the Lord'" (Ps 122:1). In response families would make last minute preparations and then begin the journey amid song, perhaps much like modern families setting off eagerly for a long-awaited vacation. Some of the psalm songs imagined the blessings of rain falling upon wadi

---

[3]R. de Vaux, *Ancient Israel: Its Life and Institutions* (Darton, Longman and Todd, 1962) 495-502.

after wadi as the pilgrims journeyed from one village or fortified town to another (68:8; 84:6-8).

As they gathered at the shrine, they became the *Qahal YHWH*, "the summoned assembly of Yahweh." The term was favored by the Priestly traditions of the Hebrew Scriptures for it emphasized that they were an interdependent community, called by the ritual sound of the *shofar*, the ram's horn, into the Divine Presence.

Upon arrival at their destination, tithes would be given to the poor or offered in sacrifice. With great practicality the later prescriptions of Deuteronomy made allowances for the conversion of local produce into money for purchasing supplies at the shrine. The convenience of carrying money rather than sheep was easily recognized as well as the way sacred laws continued to adapt to the changing economic realities of the age (Dt 14:25). At the sanctuary vows would be fulfilled, differences and arguments settled (by the ritualized casting of lots by the priest of the sanctuary if necessary), and instruction given. Some type of elementary catechesis in the religious traditions of old was provided and the great stories of Yahweh's deeds were recounted for the edification of all. By word and action the participants were once again melded into the people of God.

Sacrifices were offered to fulfill vows and to renew the great gift of the covenant. These fell into two major categories, each expressing a specific aspect of religious meaning. Some victims were totally immolated and completely consumed by the fire alone. An offering of this sort was called a holocaust, *'olah* in Hebrew, literally something "made to go upwards" in smoke and ashes. In view of the original significance of the term, its use for the enormous tragedy of the attempted Nazi extermination of the Jewish people during World War II is profound.[4]

The Book of Leviticus contains the rubrics for holocaust offerings (Lev 1:1-17). This form of sacrifice acknowledged the supreme power and authority of the Lord and prevented the subsequent reuse of the victim for personal benefit or convenience. It was offered totally and irrevocably to God alone.

The other major type of sacrifice was called a "peace offering" or "communion sacrifice,' *shelamim* in Hebrew, literally something which enhances or restores unity and peace. These were shared by the priest of the sanctuary as well as by the members of the family of the offerant. As a sacred meal, it clearly signified the restored unity among all the participants with the Lord and each other. The rubrics for this form are also carefully stipulated in the Levitical traditions for proper worship (3:1-17). Other sacrifices included "guilt offerings" ('*asham*; 5:14-26) which were later invoked as an explanation for the misfortunes of the Suffering Servant (Is 53:10) or "cereal offerings" (*Korban*; Lev 2:1-16). Each type of sacrificial offering had its own prescriptions and attendant ceremonies.

Through these various sacrificial rites and festivities peace and unity were reestablished; the covenant and its blessings were restored. The ancient stories of Yahweh's saving deeds were retold and all the present experiences became yet another chapter in the magnificent saga of divine deliverance and protection. They were liberated, not only from the slavery and oppression of Egypt, but also from their own sins. The blessing of peace was celebrated for the city of Jerusalem (Ps 122:6-9) and upon each pilgrim family (128:5-6) as they returned home amid songs of *shalom*. God had blessed his people once more. Like a beneficent Lord, Yahweh had fed them; like a cherishing mother, God nourished them for the rigors of life until the next harvest festival. The more wealthy among them had been more lavish, but no one should have been left out of the festive circle of covenant members.

The Genius of Hosea

"Since she has not known that it was I who gave her the grain, the wine, and the oil, and her abundance of silver and of gold which they used for Baal, therefore I will take back my grain in its time and my wine in its season" (Hos 2:10-11).

As centuries went by, each of the three major festivals also became associated with a major faith-event in the history of the Hebrew nation. The celebration of Unleavened Bread and Passover, for example, was immediately related to the Exodus, and for obvious reasons. The agricultural origins of the cycle of new yeast for bread from fresh grain and the nomadic roots of the practice of sacrificing lambs for protection on the occasion of movement to Spring pastures both highlighted new beginnings. The first Spring harvest at Pentecost became associated with the gift of Torah at Sinai, probably simply because of the symbolic time lapse which represented forty years in the wilderness and a period of ritual preparation for the feast. The rough huts at the time of the final Autumn harvest served to recall the tents of the wilderness and the Lord's beneficent protection during those years of wandering which received the blessing of fruitfulness as Israel took possession of the promised land.

Still the agricultural origins of each festival made these celebrations prime candidates for the celebration of fertility cults as well! Throughout the entire Ancient Near East, with only minor variations in names and dramatic detail, the succession of seasons was explained by a common myth. For each civilization the vital force of fertility in field, flock and family became the object of religious ritual and prayer. The bull was a ready symbol for the fertility desired by all. Grain and herds were needed for survival and an abundance of children provided a stable source for workers as well as eventual care in old age or infirmity.

In the myth as recounted in Canaan, the god of life and fertility (Baal) was slain by the god of death (Mot) each year as the rains ceased and the patchy fields gradually turned to brown. With the first rains in the Fall came the announcement that Baal was alive again and the blessings of new life became evident once more. It seemed so natural for farmers and shepherds to participate in rituals which initiated and shared in the deeper current of natural fertility. Sexuality became the "sacrament" of new life. Temple prostitutes enabled fragile human beings to encounter and participate in the surging power of fertility against the obstacles of drought, heat and sterility. Sexual rituals in the fields at times of planting and harvest symbolized the power of life and somehow inaugurated and assured the next phase in the annual cycle. Terra cotta images of the mother earth goddess, pregnant and bursting with new life, have been found everywhere. Poles representing sacred trees, symbols of the goddess Asherah (literally the Hebrew word for "blessing"), were also proliferated everywhere. Any green tree became a symbol for fertility, as the prophets regularly lamented (Hos 4:13). A variety of human needs on several levels converged to make the ritual and the way of life very appealing indeed. It provided an attractive explanation for life. Our modern preoccupation with sexuality and "the good life," especially as reflected in the advertisements of the day, are not far from the mentality of Canaan in this regard. When Israel or Judah gathered at festival time, however, the syncretistic mixing of Yahwism and the fertility cults was very easy indeed. All too often, at least in the common thinking of the pilgrims, Yahweh and Baal changed places.

Elijah had fought this tendency on Mount Carmel when he entered into his life and death struggle with Queen Jezebel and her prophets of Baal. They were staunch devotees of an entire way of life which gave meaning to their world, but Elijah mocked their Baal (1 K 18:27), wondering aloud if the god's silence and refusal to act occurred because Baal was sleeping or perhaps had stepped out for a moment (to relieve himself!). By contrast, Yahweh's fiery response to Elijah's sacrifice and his prompt gift of rain after a drought of over three years demonstrated that Yahweh alone was the source of fertility and life (vv. 38-39.45).

Unfortunately the message had been forgotten all too quickly. It was Hosea who merits the credit for confronting the matter in a new way, taking the bull by the horns so to speak, and rendering the symbol impotent, at least on a theological level. In the middle of the eighth century B.C.E., when prosperity (for the few) was a new way of life, and foreign merchants and traders (not to mention royal wives and their retinues) a familiar sight in the northern kingdom, when the cult of fertility had become so popular and widespread again, Hosea appeared on the scene. He would seem to be the only authentic prophet from the north whose preaching has been preserved for our generation.

The method chosen by Hosea for his new polemics was very simple and very daring. Using all the images of fertile field and marriage he applied them to Yahweh alone. In a sense he did what everyone else was doing, namely acknowledged the unifying concept of sexuality and fertility but he ascribed it all to the Lord of the covenant and made the fertility subordinate to works of justice and mercy. Unrecognized for his generosity,

Yahweh uses the prophet to announce that it will all be taken back. In the name of the Lord, Hosea states, "I will lay waste her vines and fig trees, of which she said, 'These are the hire my lovers have given me'; I will turn them into rank growth and wild beasts shall devour them" (Hos 2:14). Even more shockingly, Hosea dared to speak of Yahweh as a faithful and ardent lover of Israel, courting the nation as one might court a young bride again, enticing her into the desert for a second honeymoon in justice, love, mercy and fidelity (vv. 21-22). Though we have no record of opposition to Hosea, the ultra-orthodox of his day must have been outraged. This was not the proper way to speak of the Lord!

In his thoroughness, Hosea even carries his imagery to the point of comparing the piety and devotion of Israel to the very mists and dew of fertility which vanish the very instant they feel the heat of the morning sun (6:4). In describing the perversity of Israel, Hosea notes that "for wine and wheat they lacerated themselves" in the fashion of those who saw their own blood as a bearer of life, "while they rebelled against me" (7:14). Since it is the Lord alone who is supreme, Hosea warns that "threshing floor and wine press shall not nourish them" and "the new wine shall fail them" (9:2). Ephraim "is stricken, their root is dried up, they shall bear no fruit" (v. 16). Again and again the images of fertility are used in daring description and in novel interpretation of the bitter fruits of that age.

The impact of this theological interpretation of Hosea was not only felt by his immediate audience. A century later Jeremiah invoked the same imagery, recalling the early devotion of Israel like a newly wed bride in the desert (Jer 2:1) who became a prostitute "under every green tree" (v. 20) and a "frenzied she-camel in heat" galloping after mates (vv. 23-25). Ezekiel continued the theme, using language which bordered on coarseness to describe the affection of the Lord for Israel and the way the people seemed to delight in sexual liaisons with Egypt and Babylon (Ez 16; 23). This entire tradition formed the remote background for early Christian writers who attempted to describe the love of Christ for the Church.

Prophetic Judgment On Worship

"I hate, I spurn your feasts, I take no pleasure in your solemnities; your cereal offerings I will not accept, nor consider your stall-fed peace offerings. Away with your noisy songs! I will not listen to the melodies of your harps, but if you would offer me holocausts, then let justice surge like water, and goodness like an unfailing stream" (Am 5:21-24).

In recent years we have become familiar with the evaluation of liturgy by trained experts and volunteers. We have come to expect parish committees to assess the effectiveness of acoustics and music, the contribution of the environment or the quality of participation. Nevertheless, we are taken aback by the level at which the critique of the prophets operated in the eighth and seventh centuries B.C.E.

If worship in Israel or any other nation is intended as an expression of a people united in mutual concern and common effort, such worship is an utter travesty when built upon social injustice or lack of compassion for the suffering members of the same group. If worship in Israel or any other nation is intended as an expression of a people humbled before their god, such worship is idolatry if centered upon the arrogant power and lavish ritual of merely human actions. It was precisely these two profound flaws which pre-exilic prophets observed in the worship of the great shrines of the northern and southern kingdoms. Their criticism was biting, but their contemporary liturgical experts refused to accept their conclusion.

No matter what the response, the prophets spoke their piece clearly and boldly. They spoke in the name of the living God of the covenant to whom all worship was in fact addressed. At times the prophets spoke with bitterness, even paraphrasing the actual words used in their liturgy to illustrate the reality they witnessed.

Thus for example, Amos stood in the sanctuary of Bethel, the ancient shrine associated with Abraham (Gen 12:8) and the vision of Jacob (28:10-19), and sarcastically called, "Come to Bethel and sin, to Gilgal and sin more. . . . Proclaim publicly your free will offerings, for so you love to do, O men of Israel, says the Lord God" (Am 4:4-5). The words seem to have been based upon the wording of introductions and liturgical invitations very familiar to people who frequented the shrine. The power of the words of Amos can only be appreciated if one imagines a modern eucharistic service beginning with the priestly invitation, "As we prepare to celebrate these sacred mysteries, let us pause to sin. . . ." Startled and angry worshippers would have understood the critique of Amos only too well! He had taken a familiar phrase and deftly turned it against his own people.

Hosea likewise spoke against the worship practiced by his northern friends and neighbors, observing "though they offer sacrifice, immolate flesh and eat it, the Lord is not pleased with them" (Hos 8:13). In a play on words he also changed the name of Bethel, literally "House of God," to Bethaven which means "House of iniquity" (4:15). In several places Hosea adds damning judgments regarding the famous shrine of Gilgal which marked the place where Joshua and the Hebrews crossed the Jordan and entered the promised land. In the eyes of Hosea it was the beginning of reprobation, not election, for he stated, "all their wickedness is in Gilgal; yes, there they incurred my hatred" (9:15). Bitter words for what was venerated as a place of grace and gratitude among the generations of his day!

In words similar to those of Amos at the northern shrine of Bethel, Isaiah addressed harsh indictments in Jerusalem against the citizens of Zion whom he names with the insulting title of "princes of Sodom" and "people of Gomorrah" (Is 1:10). Stating that the Lord has "had enough of whole-burnt rams" (v. 11), the prophet ordered his listeners to "trample my courts no more" and "bring no more worthless offerings" (v. 13) for their incense made the Lord nauseous and their hands spread in prayer were revealed as "full of the blood" of the poor (v. 15). Like Amos in the citation placed at the beginning of this section, Isaiah counters with the command, "make justice your aim: redress the wronged, hear the orphan's plea, defend the widow" (v. 16). Widows and orphans were the traditional representatives of desperate people at the margins of their world and dependent on the help of others for survival. The entire passage from Isaiah, like that of Amos, is well worth pondering in all its forceful language.

Jeremiah brought the message of Isaiah to full term by announcing that the Temple, established by Solomon as a sign of Divine Presence, would be destroyed just as Shiloh had been destroyed by the Philistines some four centuries earlier (1 Sam 1:9; 4:3-22). Jeremiah pronounced a famous mimicry of the prayers of Temple worshipers who repeated "Temple of the Lord, Temple of the Lord, Temple of the Lord" (Jer 7:4) while continuing to oppress the poor, murder and steal, commit adultery and perjury and worship strange and alien gods (vv. 5-10). For this bold speech Jeremiah was beaten and placed in stocks overnight by Pashhur the priest (20:1-2). For his efforts to protect the reputation of the great shrine, Pashhur in turn was given the name "Terror on every Side" by Jeremiah, and the priest was promised exile or death for himself and all his friends at the hands of the Babylonians (vv3-6)! But they would not pay the price of conversion entailed in truly listening to the invective of the prophet. As a result the entire complex was demolished by the very armies named by Jeremiah (2 K 25:8-17).

Two famous citations from pre-exilic prophets illustrate the highest priorities of the God of Israel's covenant, especially in regard to the public worship so dear to the Semitic hearts of the people. Hosea summed it up by affirming, "It is love (*hesed*) that I desire, not sacrifice (*zabah*), and knowledge (*da'at*) of God rather than holocausts (*'olot*)" (Hos 6:6). For Hosea community bonds and mutual concern were more important in the eyes of the Lord than immolated victims, and the intimate union of the human family with their God more significant for worship than the ritual burning of sacrificial gifts. For Hebrews the notion of "knowledge" was far more comprehensive than mere intellectual comprehension. It included genuine concern and affection as evidenced by the way it was used for the physical expression of the bond between husband and wife (Gen 4:25). It is a curious fact that the same word is also used in the modern state of Israel to designate the government office of the Department of Religion (*da'at*) charged with the responsibilities of overseeing the activities of the various religious communities in the nation.

Likewise the prophet Micah, a contemporary of Isaiah, raised the question of what truly was pleasing to God above all else. Is it "thousands of rams" or "myriad streams of oil?" Is it

even so personal a precious a gift as the sacrifice of a first born
(Mic 6:7)? Micah set the record straight with his memorable
response. "You have been told, o earthling (*Adam*), what is
good and what the Lord requires of you: only to do the right
(*mishpat*), to love fidelity (*hesed*) and to walk humbly with
your God" (v. 8). For Micah and the entire prophetic tradition
canonized in the inspired collection of Scripture, the message
remained constant. Just customs, mutual concern and humble
pilgrimage with God represent the only basis upon which
acceptable worship can be built. Liturgy without social consciousness or worship without social action renders ritual
merely an empty performance. Such liturgy was as unacceptable to the prophets of Israel as it would be to modern
Christian disciples of the Prophet from Nazareth.

※

Three questions from the prophets for the appendix of
every order of true worship:

Are the most marginal members of the worshipping assembly truly welcomed and respected or are they somehow
"taken advantage of" by the group's more prominent persons?

Does the "geiger counter" of prophetic justice find any
trace of exploitation in the resources used in a given liturgy?

Is every member of the worshipping assembly inspired to
work for the Lord's justice as a result of the renewal of
covenant inherent in each gathering?

6

Messengers Of Judgment

It has often been observed that the rise of the great classical pre-exilic prophets coincided with a new task in Israel and Judah its southern neighbor, namely the burden of announcing judgment and rejection of the entire nation. Such was not an easy responsibility, and may have contributed to the fact that prophetic oracles, earlier termed "the word of the Lord," later became described as "a burden from the Lord" (Mal 1:13). The task of saying hard things may indeed be a burden in any age. The early prophets were no exception. They announced the judgment of God upon institutions they had cherished.

Negative judgments had been uttered by prophets from the beginning of the monarchy. Samuel rejected Saul from the kingship for his lack of obedience (1 Sam 13:13; 15:22-31) and Nathan denounced the adultery of David in no uncertain terms through the touching parable of the special lamb (2 Sam 12:1-12). The prophet Ahijah ripped his new cloak into twelve pieces and gave ten to Jeroboam, promising that he would rule over ten tribes in Israel after the schism at the death of Solomon (1 K 11:26-43). It was the partial rejection of Rehoboam, son of Solomon. Elijah described the punishment which would fall upon the head of Ahab for being an accomplice to Jezebel's bloody elimination of Naboth (21:17-26). The full effect of the judgment was postponed due to the humble penance of Ahab (vv. 27-29), but the punishment eventually fell upon the royal house as the prophet had promised. In each case a prophet had confronted the king with indictment and verdict. The unique and novel dimension of the prophets whose words were collected and written down stemmed from the fact that they rejected the entire nation in the name of the Lord God. For a nation whose very existence was based upon the spiritual reality of a convenantial bond, it was a terrifying word to hear!

The message itself was powerful and alarming, but the literary form used by these prophetic messengers was also capable of capturing the attention of those who heard it in the Temple courtyard or city gate. Just as our modern society instinctively constructs communication in different ways according to its purpose, so also did ancient Israel develop specific patterns for individual human situations.

We readily recognize the distinctive oral components of a television commercial, even when we can't see the screen, for each message includes something to catch our attention, to convince us of our pressing need for the object and to underscore the irresistibility of the price. An expression of sympathy is obviously very different, or the stylized communication familiar from liturgy or courtroom. We have only to hear the words and the basic sequence of ideas in order to identify instinctively the social context within which such communication would be appropriate. We easily distinguish public language from family table talk, or the speech of a lawyer from that of a theologian, business reports from parish council discussions. Listen to little children at play as they mimic parents, teachers or clergy and learn something of the language patterns of our culture. They note what scholars conclude, namely that the form of speech, the sequence of ideas and the vocabulary disclose the original context and purpose of our speech.

The same measurements can be applied to the modes of communication used in ancient Israel and Judah.[1] As an oral society with apparently little dependence on the written word in daily life, the basic forms of speech were highly refined and easily recognized. The language of the Temple as well as that of the justice system practiced at the city gate were quite distinctive. The prophets knew those patterns and so did their contemporaries. As noted in the previous chapter, the prophets sometimes parodied the language of worship in their critique of the same. They also borrowed the language used by village elders and princes in rendering judgment upon the guilty. Those who spoke in the name of the Lord used language people would understand.

The formal structure of judgment is simple. In its full form it consists in the statement of the crime, an indication of the authority or competence in the matter, and the announcement of the punishment which is always somehow related to the nature of the crime committed. The section dealing with the crime as well as that pronouncing the penalty may be amplified and more elaborately described in some cases. This is the form most frequently encountered in the passages preserved for us from the speeches of the pre-exilic prophets.

Judgment on the Nation

> *"Proclaim this in the castles of Ashdod,*
> *in the castles of the land of Egypt:*

[1] For a full introduction to biblical literary forms, consult the classic study by K. Koch, *The Growth of the Biblical Tradition* (Scribner's, 1969).

> 'Gather about the mountain of Samaria,
>   and see the great disorders within her,
>   the oppression in her midst.'
> For they know not how to do what is right,
>   says the Lord,
> Storing up in their castles
>   what they have extorted and robbed.
> Therefore, thus says the Lord God:
> An enemy shall surround the land,
>   and strip you of your strength,
>   and pillage your castles ' (Am 3:9-11).

As one sent to utter judgment upon the entire nation, Amos was forced to confront the people with their crimes. Like all persons who come close to the reality of God, the sins and evil of their lives and world become brutally evident, and they are forced by inner honesty to proclaim the truth of things, no matter whom they may offend. Thus Amos was forced to echo the roar of the angry judging God (1:2; 3:8). The text cited in full above represents one of the many expressions of that Divine verdict found in the collected oracles of Amos. They were all presumably uttered in the courtyard of the sanctuary at Bethel or in relation to the people who gathered there.

The oracle begins with a public notice of trial sent to the neighboring Philistines and Egyptians. As ancient traditional enemies, they are summoned to witness the sovereign action of Yahweh and the ensuing humiliation of the northern kingdom of Israel. Those very nations who had been defeated earlier by the Lord's power were now invited to be present for the tragic downfall of Israel. The invitation is addressed, not to the common folk or to the sanctuary attendants of their gods, but to the castles of the land as symbols for the royal exercise of political power and commercial enterprise. Enemies who had once learned all too bitterly of the Lord's power on behalf of his servants, were now to witness the sad results of serving that same Lord poorly. They are invited to the very hill upon which the capital city of Samaria stood with all its palaces and walls. They were summoned to act as formal legal witnesses and spectators for the fate of Samaria and the royal sanctuary of Bethel some thirty miles away (originally built close to Jerusalem to seduce people away from the Temple there). The precise object to which their attention was directed by the Lord as plaintiff and sovereign judge was the gross social disorder and oppression practiced in the city (3:9).

As noted in the oracle cited above, there follows a brief description of the crime of the accused, namely the general lack of concern for doing what is right, and the specific allegation of storing stolen property in the castles of Samaria (v. 10). The audience knew first hand of the many artistic works of art and the special treasures of the rich citizens of that city. Some have been excavated and remain priceless acquisitions in the museums of the world. The inlaid ivory furniture and exquisite pottery are primary examples. Everything is catalogued by the prophet and labeled "stolen" and the entire city is therefore placed under judgment. The evidence is available to the observation of everyone and stands on its own merit as placed before the Divine court. It is the concluding judgment which bears the thunder of the Word of the Lord.

With the famous phrase, "thus says (literally "said" as if the Lord's very speaking already produced the effect and accomplished the purpose) the Lord," Amos announced a punishment exactly fashioned to fit the crime. An enemy will lay siege to the town, remove the fortifications (in Hebrew as in English, the word "strength" or "fortification" is often an abstract term for the stone walls themselves), and destroy the very palaces built to house the ill-gotten gain (v. 11). The ancient palaces of Egypt and Ashdod will stand in awe of this great reversal in fate.

The entire literary form of judgment as familiar from the judicial practices of the city gates was present in the announcement of Amos: crime, judicial authority and punishment. An additional note in the text illustrates the extent of the promised destruction, as Israelites dwelling in Samaria are described desperately snatching the corner of a couch or cot in a futile attempt to save some small useless reminder of the past (v. 12). Enemy governments watch the total collapse of those who forgot their power was completely dependent upon their respect for the Lord and their protection of the poor. The nation was doomed and Amos was delegated to announce that fact.

A smaller segment of the citizenry of Samaria received a similar message of judgment and destruction from Amos. One by one he singles out those who must bear the terrible consequences of the nation's crime. Among these groups are the wealthy women of the city, sarcastically called "cows of Bashan" (4:1). The prophet commanded them to listen/obey the word he was about to proclaim, and by his announcement Amos was intending to initiate the very judgment he pronounced. With poetic insight and parody Amos compared the prominent women of the capital to the sleek cattle which grazed on the rich pastures across the Jordan. It was the dairyland of the area and the cattle were the paragon of contented existence. The crime of these women is underscored by Amos as oppressing the weak and abusing the needy, and then casually requesting a refreshing drink from their husbands in utter unconcern for the exploitation and injustice outside their latticed windows. They were indifferent to the pitiful reality at their doorsteps, almost like cattle blissfully ignorant of surrounding human needs. The indignant and holy God vowed to intervene (v. 2) and the dire penalty is announced by Amos. Since these women have acted like cattle, they will be treated as such. They will be dragged away with hooks in hair, ears or nose through destroyed city walls and into the mire, "says the Lord" (v. 3). Again and again the punishment fits the crime and bears the awful weight of divine authority and power. The women are singled out as a major force in leadership and share the fate of the entire nation. Once again the judicial form is present in the announcement: introduction, accusation open to the testimony of everyone, invocation of Divine authority and intervention followed by the imposition of the well deserved punishment.

Sanctuary priests also shared in the punishment proclaimed by Amos, and Amaziah of Bethel became the representative for the entire group. In refusing to listen to Amos' dire words against his royal master, Amaziah committed the terrible crime of stifling prophecy and muzzling the preaching of Amos (7:16). Because he refused to submit to the Word of the Lord in the words of Amos, his family would be forced to pay the price of experiencing the very events about which the prophet tried to warn: his wife would become a desperate prostitute in a destroyed city, his children slain, his land lost, and he would eventually die in a foreign land of exile (v. 17). All this surged into full view when the Assyrian armies finally captured Samaria and reduced the kingdom to provincial status after the dreadful siege of the city in 721 B.C.E. The prophet Amos saw it all on the horizon about to break into human history, but the priests refused to allow such nonsense and disloyalty to be spoken. In another passage Amos returns to the crime of stifling prophecy and announces the penalty for the nation, namely a terrible famine for the word of God

(8:11-12). Those who make fun of prayer are sometimes punished by the inability to do so in moments of desperate need; those who dismiss prophecy as empty wind find the same when they seek substance. Because the punishment almost invariably fits the crime, the thoughtful reader is invited to seek the connection in every prophetic oracle of judgment. It becomes a journey into the mind and spirituality of the prophets.

The same message is repeated throughout the book of Amos. Because of the crimes of oppression (5:12), for example, the wailing and lament shall not merely be heard among the poor victims but will fill the fields and vineyards with bitter echoes (vv. 16-17). Elsewhere the Lord swears never to forget what they have done (8:7). The same final judgment was spoken by Amos against the Temple itself, promising that the elaborately and delicately carved columns would be shattered and the inhabitants slain in their flight (9:1)! Even if they should attempt to hide in the very heavens or under the sea, they would be struck down, for the Lord had fixed his terrible gaze upon them "for evil and not for good" (v. 4)!

The entire nation had been judged and found wanting. As a recipient of benefits and covenant partner with the Lord, they were condemned by the very standards accepted when the covenant was inaugurated. The curses which were part of every Ancient Near Eastern agreement had now been released to take their effect, and Amos was destined to be the bearer of that bad news. A remnant may remain, like the edge of the couch (3:12), but of the hundred people who march forth in arrogance only ten will survive (5:3). Only a few will be left to carry out the dead (6:10).

Although Amos seems to have been the first voice lifted in declaring the end of the nation, he was not alone in this terrible task. Hosea pulls the nation into a formal law suit, accusing the people of serious crimes: "no fidelity (*'emet* which is also translated as "truth" or "stability"), no mercy (*hesed*), no knowledge (*da'at*) of God in the land. False swearing, lying, murder, stealing and adultery" (Hos 4:1-2)! With an insight and vengance which would make a modern environmentalist both rejoice and shudder, the punishment becomes the reversal of all of creation and the destruction of beasts, birds and fish (v. 3).

Hosea also singles out the clergy of his day for special doses of divine retribution. Because the priests have rejected knowledge (*da'at*) with all the dimensions of interpersonal concern and affection inherent in the Hebrew term, they are rejected from the priesthood itself, which is based upon the presumption of such a reciprocal bond (4:6). Since they have ignored the instruction (*torah*) of God, that same God will ignore their children and refuse to give them the teaching which was a sign of care and responsibility. Hosea asserted that the priests fed on the sin and guilt of the people (v.8), benefitting from the guilt offerings stipulated as penance for sin and encouraging a sense of guilt. Since they received a portion of each victim for their own sustenance and for the support of their families according to the levitical tradition in Israel, the prophet denounced their inclination to maintain guilt for selfish reasons rather than out of genuine concern for the holiness of the Lord. The judgment remains a bitter pill for pastoral personnel of all ages!

Isaiah also has long passages preserving the poetic judgment which he announced to the people of Zion and Jerusalem. The community subsequently judged these passages to be the Word of God for all time, universal in application and simply too important to forget! Because Isaiah saw the city filled with fortune-tellers and idols (Is 2:6-7), they shall face a judgment so terrible that they will cringe and crouch in the dust behind rocks "from the terror of the Lord and the splendor of his majesty" (vv. 10. 19. 21). Woe after woe was announced (5:8. 11. 18. 20. 21. 22) to all the various persons and groups guilty of injustice. Those who collect real estate would find their houses in ruin and uninhabited (vv. 8-10) as yet another example of the punishment befitting the crime. Since it was the entire nation which bore the brunt of Isaiah's judgment, the punishment found expression in the Lord calling a foreign nation as one might whistle for a dog which comes running in prompt response (vv. 26-29). They will come, says Isaiah in the name of the Lord, without weariness and stumbling, without broken sandals, with bent bows and sharpened arrows. They would come like a hurricane or a roaring lion. Thus the judgment announced by Isaiah.

Jeremiah joins the chorus of those announcing the end of the nation. In a magnificent poem revealing all the skill of a consummate artist, Jeremiah describes the experience of the march of the Babylonian army through the land. In sharp staccato phrases, the prophet recounts the wail of lamenters, the terror of the royal court, the trumpets of battle, the dust of the chariots, pounding heartbeats of fear, the smashing of tents and the utter ruin of city after city (4:5-21). The end result is the total reversal of creation, with the earth reverting to "waste and void" (*tohu webohu*), the lights of heaven extinguished, the hills crumbling into dust, the removal of Earthling (*adam*), the birds flown away, and the gardens turning into ruin and dust once more (vv. 23-26). Again and again Jeremiah warned king Zedekiah that there would be no escape from the hands of the Babylonians (34:2-3; 38:17-18).

Just as the earlier words of judgment found final expression in the destruction of Samaria by the Assyrians, so this series found fulfillment in the ruin of Jerusalem (39:1-7). The generals forced Zedekiah to witness the murder of his sons before being blinded so that he would forever carry the memory of that final brutal experience. It was a terrible disaster for people and leaders as they marched off to exile in 587 B.C.E. The word spoken by the prophets was the beginning of reality, not a mere preface. The burden of pre-exilic prophecy was to announce the very painful message of the end of the nation. The Deuteronomic covenant was conditional. It depended upon the obedience of the people of Israel. While the Lord could establish a new relationship by his sovereign and gracious will, the first was ended.

Prophetic Signs and Actions

"Then the Lord said, 'Just as my servant Isaiah has gone naked and barefoot for three years as a sign and portent against Egypt and Ethiopia, so shall the king of Assyria lead away captives from Egypt and exiles from Ethiopia young and old, naked and barefoot, with buttocks uncovered!'" (Is 20:3-4).

The prophets of Israel could never be contented with mere words, for speech had to overflow into action. Moreover, the words of their lips were powerful and effective. Any human speech in the oral society of Irsael was perceived to achieve its effect. Spoken agreements became reality and blessings or curses could not be withdrawn. The blessings of Isaac for Jacob and Esau (Gen 27:1-40) had long been a witness to the power of the spoken word, and the judgments of the prophets continued in the same vein. Still, actions are the inevitable complement of speech and the symbolic gestures of the prophets were very significant for their message of judgment.

Each prophetic action inaugurated the reality it signified. The symbolic actions of the prophets of Israel were viewed with fear and dismay, for they symbolized and initiated the judgment and penalty which the pre-exilic prophets were sent to announce.

Those who ponder the words of prophets should also see their lives as a significant dimension of their message. A brief review of the major actions will illustrate the point. When Elijah promised a daily supply of food and oil for the poor widow, he was inaugurating the salvation he promised to those who remained generous to prophets and faithful to the Lord, even in the dire straits of the famine (1 K 17:7-16). The water poured over the sacrifice on Carmel (18:34) was the beginning of rain for the famished and thirsty land. His task had been to promise salvation to those who remained faithful and zealous in the service of the Lord.

The task of the majority of pre-exilic prophets, as we have seen above, was a more negative mission. The destruction they affirmed was accomplished by signs which underscored and inaugurated the deadly reality. Although we have no such action from the life of Amos, we do have the memory of Hosea's marriage to the cult prostitute as vivid judgment and indictment against the fickle nature of the nation's covenantal loyalty (Hos 1:2). His entire life became the medium of the message, and thus he became a pattern for those who would come after him claiming to speak in the name of the Lord. Life reflects message or reduces it to meaningless mimicry.

It may have been a bit chilly if Isaiah did in fact walk the streets of Jerusalem for three years without sackcloth around his waist or sandals on his feet (Is 20:2). The mental image of a naked and barefoot prophet going about his daily errands may strike a comic note for modern readers, but the realization that this both symbolized and initiated the humiliating exile of Egypt and Ethiopia was received with alarm by those who witnessed the reality however long it may have existed. Similarly, the poultice of fig paste applied by Isaiah to the ailing king Hezekiah was not a miracle drug or magic incantation, but rather the beginning of salvation announced for the entire nation in the face of Assyria's threatened destruction. The fidelity of Hezekiah temporarily averted further destruction and the medicine initiated the provisional cure of the nation, at least for the time being (38:6-9. 21-22).

Prophetic actions seem to have increased as the danger to the nation came closer, for the book of Jeremiah abounds with such accounts. The rotten loin cloth was presented as the beginning of the rottenness of the entire nation (Jer 13:1-11). It was more than a character slur; it was the revelation of the deeper reality in the eyes of the prophet! His own celibacy as commanded by the Lord (16:1-4) became the vivid reminder of the future when all would find themselves without wives or children in the face of Babylonian reprisals. His own life began what others would be forced to experience for their refusal to hear. Jeremiah also watched a potter and turned the potter's effort to reshape the wet soft clay into the beginning of the Lord's reshaping divine plans for the destiny of Israel (18:1-12). Moreover, his smashing of the potter's vessel was intended to be the beginning of the destruction of the entire city, irreparably strewn across the ground into so many fragments (19:1-15). Jeremiah also fashioned and wore a yoke as the prophetic beginning of the submission which all of Judah would be forced to experience at the hands of the king of Babylon (27:1-8). Another prophet, Hananiah by name, roughly took the yoke from Jeremiah and broke it as the welcome sign of a more positive reality (28:10-11), but after a time of inner uncertainty Jeremiah returned with a yoke of iron as the final word (vv. 12-14). Hananiah scoffed, but Jeremiah peered into the truth of the situation and announced Hananiah's death, which occurred in the seventh month of the same year (vv. 15-17)! The actions produced the reality, and Hananiah's own demise became the beginning of the destruction which all would eventually experience, for the Lord had decreed it.

After the first exile invoked upon the citizens of Jerusalem by Babylon in 597/6 B.C.E., Ezekiel probably viewed the final demise of the city from a distance. He was among the cream of the city's society which had been forced into exile in retaliation for their rebellion. As a prophet of the Lord, Ezekiel knew that the destruction announced by so many others was an inevitable reality and his actions illustrated the destiny of Jerusalem seen from across the great rivers of Babylon. He was struck dumb (Ez 3:26-27), possibly in the sense that he could speak only God's word, uttering nothing from his own heart. At least that interpretation enables the reader to understand the symbolic gesture in view of the fact that some thirty chapters of the book pass before the reader receives word of the arrival of the messenger with the news of the fall of Jerusalem (33:21-22)! Poor Ezekiel is forced by divine command to scratch an outline of the city under siege as the beginning of the enemies' plans to destroy everything (4:1), to commence a fast like those living under siege (v. 9) and to cook his food over human excrement like those in dire poverty within the city walls (v. 12). He is required to shave his head and beard, burning a third of the hair as the beginning of the blaze in Jerusalem, as he announced to the bystanders, "This is Jerusalem" (5:5). He was forbidden to mourn at the death of his beloved wife as the first stoic response to the destruction of the beloved city of

Jerusalem. Poor Ezekiel was even ordered to pack his belongings like a refugee, and in the presence of bewildered neighbors told to dig a hole in the wall and crawl through as the beginning of the exile for those back in Jerusalem. Those who witnessed these actions were very angry for they understood each gesture as the ritual beginning of the realities they presignaled!

All of these symbolic actions form the background for that final gesture of the Prophet from Nazareth when he broke bread with his disciples as the solemn prophetic inauguration of the brokenness of his life for their sakes.

Violence

> "I cry out to you, 'Violence!' but you do not intervene"
> (Hab 1:2).

The reality of violence has a long history in biblical tradition. The cataclysmic destruction of the evil generations at the time of Noah for example (Gen 7:1-5), represented the violent attempt of God to purify the earth at the time of the great deluge. The gift of human freedom survived with Noah's family, and the cycle of the violence of one person toward another began again. The Exodus was marked by the unleashing of the great plagues against ancient Egypt as a result of the hardened heart of Pharaoh who refused freedom to the Hebrews. That violence was in retribution for the cruel treatment of the Hebrew slaves by the royal foremen who increased the quota of bricks without providing additional straw (Ex 5:6-21). The violent intervention of the Lord became a God-given means of escape and liberation. Amos continued along this line by invoking the violence of fire and destruction against the city ramparts of those nations which practiced violence against their neighbors in an inhumane fashion. Included among the nations threatened with such violence for their violations of "human rights" were Aram, Philistia, Tyre, Edom, Ammon, and Moab (Am 1:3-2:3) to which list Israel was added much to the chagrin of the prophet's audience (2:6-16), and then Judah as the Babylonians came upon the scene in judgment (vv. 4-5).

Violence for violence was threatened by Amos against those in Israel whose homes were built by exploitation (Am 3:10) and Zephaniah promised punishment for those "who fill the house of their master with violence and deceit" (Zeph 1:9). The principle of "an eye for an eye, tooth for a tooth, hand for hand, foot for foot, burn for burn, wound for wound" (Ex 21:24-25; Lev 24:17-22) is brought to bear by the prophets on those who indulge in wanton disregard for the dignity of their covenantal partners or the material gifts which those partners had received. In the eyes of the prophets, those who appropriate the goods of others cavalierly will themselves become the target of divine judgment. The purpose was to balance the scales in favor of people who remained faithful under adversity. The judgment of God evened the score and reversed the injustice of this age. The judgment of God also took the standard from humanity and applied it evenly. It was this same principle which was invoked by the Prophet from Galilee who warned, "the measure with which you measure will in return be measured out to you" (Lk 6:38).

The prophets repeatedly suggest that the phrase "violence and destruction" was a common slogan or warning in their public speeches. The words may even have been among the phrases borrowed from judicial trials and used regularly in pre-exilic prophetic denunciations. Jeremiah spoke of "violence and destruction" (Jer 6:7) resounding in the streets, and Habakkuk cries out "violence" but the Lord seemingly refused

to intervene for the time being (Hab 2:1) even though the land
suffered from violence (2:8.17). Even priests are denounced
for doing violence to the law by Zephaniah (Zeph 3:4). Fair
warning was given to all of those who were about to experience
the brunt of the Lord's even-handed punishment.

One might suggest three sources for the violence reflected
in pre-exilic prophetic literature. One source for the violence
is the utter disregard of the wealthy and prominent for the
rights of the poor. Another source is found in the zealous
action of the Lord of Israel in behalf of the poor and oppressed.
On occasion, as Habakkuk pointed cut in exasperation, this
occurs in a time-frame far distinct from the urgency desired by
the human heart (Hab 2:2-3); but the vision will come in its
own time. Still a third source stems from the experience of
covenantal imperatives which bring judgment, but also open
up lives to new avenues of change and conversion. While the
conversion demanded by the Lord of Israel's covenant respected human freedom, it still required a response which was
not always convenient or enjoyable, at least not initially. The
"way of the Lord" (their expression for what moderns term
"moral theology") was one of justice, mutual fidelity and
zealous devotion to the will of the Lord. The zeal of the Lord
in pursuit of a plan of salvation entailed some types of
"violence" against everything which stood in the way of peace
and justice at its deepest level. Those who upheld God's zeal
also shared in it. Yahweh and the prophet were bound
together, sometimes in the minority, as a "remnant" in a
larger, often hostile world.

The power of God was able to dominate every aspect of
that world, even the inner world of the prophet's own consciousness and human will. The God of peace was also a God
of violence, at least in some manner. The God of peace was

also a God of power and zeal. These are modern musings on the experience of the prophets before the mystery of the Lord's Person. They are also perennial.

The spirituality of an authentic prophet must come to grips with the sovereign action of Yahweh. Perhaps it was a post-exilic bit of embroidery upon the tapestry of earlier prophetic warning, but Micah is quoted as saying, "As for me, I am filled with power, with the spirit of the Lord, with authority and with might; to declare to Jacob his crimes and to Israel his sins" (Mic 3:8). A long and sometimes painful history of struggling with the divine will lead to the recognition that divine power was not against creation, but rather intended to bring out the very best of humanity which was often too short-sighted to recognize its own good at first glance.Even the destruction of the nation was the end of one reality in order to highlight the beginning of another.

Three judgments for our own day:

What radical flaw in the social values around you demands judgment today?

If crimes contain the very seeds of their own logical punishment, what type of retribution will come to the violations of the Lord's covenant still residing in your heart?

How does the violence which is splashed across every newspaper's front page fit into the covenantal and prophetic categories of this chapter?

7

Heralds Of Salvation

One of the foundational prophecies uttered in Judah was pronounced by Nathan who promised David an heir whose royal throne would last forever (2 Sam 7:1-17). Although Samuel had established Saul's reign as a grace for the nation, his approval was begrudging and temporary. David's dynasty on the other hand was pronounced as lasting forever; at least that's how Nathan saw it from the very beginning. Even if successors might deviate from the Lord's covenant, the punishment would not invalidate the relationship; after chastisement the covenant would endure. This was in contrast to the so-called Mosaic covenant as described by Deuteronomy which was always viewed as conditional. If the people obeyed, they would be God's special possession (Ex 19:3-8). Although the task given to many pre-exilic prophets was that of harsh judgment and rejection, the basic purpose for the institution of prophecy was very positive, namely the ensuring of Israel's faithful service to the Lord and the maintenance of a fruitful bond between the Lord and his people. It may even have been the sacred task of the prophet (or priests) at worship to declare the formula of covenantal bonding "I shall be their God and they shall be my people" (Jer 31:33; Ez 36:28). They were intended to be bearers of good news, not bad.

As noted before, Elijah was forced into a pessimistic mood by the conditions of his age. He could only promise salvation to the seven thousand "who had not knelt to Baal or kissed him" (1 K 19:18). Similarly Amos could only suggest the possibility of salvation for "a pair of legs or the tip of a sheep's ear" (Am 3:12) snatched from the mouth of the devouring lion. It would be a meager remnant indeed as Amos asserted again and again.

Because Hosea took to heart the anguish of God, he could not pronounce a final end to Ephraim, the tribe which represented the entire northern kingdom. Because Yahweh was "God not a human being" (Hos 11:9), Hosea continually held out the possibility of the restoration of the broken marriage bond (2:18) and the return from exile in Egypt or Assyria "like trembling sparrows" (11:11). The tenderness of Hosea's message also witnessed the growing threat from Assyria as the mighty king Tiglath-pileser III (745-727 B.C.E.) and his successors expanded to conquer vast portions of the Ancient Near East. Exile and systematic replacement by foreign groups was Assyria's preferred method of squelching attempted rebellion. Hosea knew that some exile was inevitable if Assyria's armies were successful, but his affection for the people of the land would not allow the prophet to be completely negative about future prospects. In some way the Lord would restore his people.

As the text stands today, some hint of salvation can be read in the midst of the rejection of sanctuary worship at Bethel, for Amos is cited as promising pity on the remnant of Joseph if they would "hate evil and love good" (5:15). Perhaps true liturgy could turn the tide, but Amos was not too sanguine about the realistic prospects of such a development.

Return of the Northern Kingdom

"Thus says the Lord: In Ramah is heard the sound of mourning, of bitter weeping! Rachel mourns her children, she refuses to be consoled because her children are no more. Thus says the Lord: Cease your cries of mourning, wipe the tears from your eyes. The sorrow you have shown shall have its reward, says the Lord, they shall return from the enemy's land" (Jer 31:15-16).

There was a sign of promised salvation in the famous oracle of the plowshares found in Isaiah 2:2-5 and Micah 4:1-5. The short stubby metal blades of swords would be converted to plowblades and pruning saws for removing dead branches. In this repeated vision of universal pilgrimage to Zion, God's holy mountain, the prophets envisioned all nations coming to Zion for instruction and worship. It may be a post-exilic addition to the pre-exilic text. The texts seem to dream of universal salvation in a fashion quite uncharacteristic of the age. As a motto for the modern institution of the United Nations, it represents a dream of many who love peace and feel its absence keenly today. The roots of this promise of universal harmony and peace indicate the fundamental positive mission enjoyed by the prophets of Israel and Judah, even if they gave strong condemnations as well.

It remained for Jeremiah, especially in the earlier years of his ministry, to announce the return of those who had been scattered at the destruction of Samaria. He described festive dancing and tambourines once more in the lush vineyards of Samaria at the time of planting (31:4-5). Jeremiah exults over the Lord's redemptive act as He leads the remnant home again, the blind and the lame, mothers with children (vv. 7-8), for in spite of everything, Ephraim remains "my first-born" (v. 9) as part of the enduring grace of the covenant. Ramah, the place of

Rachel's burial (1 Sam 10:2), is the symbol for a mother's lament for lost children. Jeremiah flings an impossible challenge, saying that only if the very heavens could be accurately measured or the depths sounded could the Lord cast off the entire race of Israel forever (Jer 31:37). It was clearly an impossible task and, therefore, Israel should check the markers on the highway home (v. 21).

Several aspects of this consoling promise from Jeremiah make it a powerful word of comfort for those seeking inner peace after an abortion. The use of the term "Project Rachel" for the community's desire to reach out in compassion gives a new depth to the dream first enunciated by Jeremiah for the return from exile!

In a later phase of Jeremiah's ministry, he turned his attention to the congenital deceitfulness of the people of Judah (5:1-5; 9:2-8), almost as if it were the original sin of the nation. He became totally absorbed by the shadow of Babylon's imminent invasion from the north (6:1-30). Still the promise of salvation remained for those of the north who had paid the price of exile for their rebellion and sins. Faithful to the theology of the Deuteronomic covenant, Jeremiah continued to hold out the possibility of return to the Lord for those who experienced inner circumcised hearts (4:4). Overshadowing that offer, however, because of the obdurate hearts of the princes, priests and people of Judah, was the threatened invasion by the Babylonian armies. Their victory was inevitable in the eyes of Jeremiah, and they would function as the purifying and renewing instrument of God's salvation. Their presence would be both judgment and salvation because those who would go off into exile were the chosen remnant, "the good figs" who will know the Lord (24:1-10). Jeremiah announced that these very people would become the cove-

nanted family of the Lord, for again they would be his people
and he would be their God (v. 7).

Penitential Rituals

"Assyria will not save us, nor shall we have horses to mount; we
shall say no more 'our God' to the work of our hands; for in you
the orphan finds compassion" (Hos 14:4).

One of the most endearing facets of the prophet Jeremiah is
found in the fact that we possess in his oracles an extraordinary
window into the very human struggles of his life. A series of
texts have received the title "confessions" because they reveal
so much of the inner turmoil associated with his task. Among
these expressions of personal anxiety and even rebellion against
the Lord we find a variety of emotions (Jer 12:1-4; 17:14-18;
20:7-18). For our purposes the most useful seems to reflect a
moment of crisis in Jeremiah's life (15:10-21). Regretting
bitterly the day of his birth (v. 10), the prophet accuses the
Lord of being like "a treacherous brook" (v. 18) whose waters
are only briefly available, but disappear in times of thirst and
need.

The response of the Lord is an invitation to conversion
(v. 19). In spite of Jeremiah's impetuous complaint, it is the
prophet who must change, not God. Restoration by God and
personal toughness against the opposition of the leaders in
Jerusalem is only promised if Jeremiah will once more sort out
the valuable elements in his life and eliminate the garbage.
Deliverance is contingent upon the prophet's fidelity and
perseverance. It is the story of a prophet's experience of
conversion and penance. Jeremiah was not absolved by his call
of renewed efforts or the acknowledgement of sin in the very

exercise of his mission. The existence of this penitential confession is very consoling indeed!

Reading through the prophetic materials, we find several passages in which the people are described as responding positively to the Lord's call for change of heart and renewed justice. Perhaps it is simply a reality of human nature that such grand expressions of renewed fidelity and promises of obedience were most frequent during periods of difficulty. While the purification of Temple worship and the removal of the high places did occur during times of great national resurgence under Hezekiah and Josiah, it was experienced even more frequently during times of military threat from foreign armies. Although atheism is a distinctly modern phenomenon which no Israelite could even imagine, the level of religious fervor certainly rose in times of distress.

Several texts seem to offer touching and sincere expressions of remorse for sin. They are presented as if the entire nation rose in unison to beg divine forgiveness for the sins of the people. When first read, they seem to offer precisely the type of response desired by the prophetic bearers of judgment. The negative divine response comes as a distinct surprise and requires some thoughtful reflection.

Early in the book of Jeremiah we encounter such a passage (3:21-25). The passage begins with a reference to plaintive weeping because the people have "perverted their ways and forgotten the Lord" (v. 21). This is followed by an acknowledgement of the deceptiveness of the hills where the fertility shrines abound, since the salvation of Israel is in the Lord alone (v. 22). Using the name of Shame for Baal, the prayer recognizes that the inheritance of the people has been devoured by Shame, which has almost become a blanket for cover each night (vv. 23-25). When the final phrase of the prayer confesses, "we listened not to the voice of the Lord, our God," it seems like a very humble response to grace. The Lord's response demands that they put their detestable things out of His sight (4:1). Apparently the one reality not mentioned in the prayer was a willingness to make changes, to do things differently; therefore it was not acceptable to the Lord. The crucial future-oriented aspect was missing. God was not impressed.

The book of Jeremiah seems to contain an abundance of such misdirected prayers of penance. Another passage stands in the midst of a description of a terrible drought in Judah (14:7-9). The lack of water produced lifeless city gates and cries of anguish in the streets of Jerusalem. Servants sent to the cisterns returned with empty jars and despairing hearts (vv. 2-3) while wild asses gasped for breath on the bare hills (v. 6). Once more the prophet records prayers of sorrow from the people who realize that their own crimes and rebellions rise in witness against them (v. 7). They address the Lord as "Hope of Israel" and "Savior in time of need" (v. 8). The act of contrition ends with a query regarding God who seems a traveler passing through the land without concern or a champion without strength to save. Once again, there is not the slightest hint of a willingness to show evidence of a change of heart; hence the Lord's response is to forbid Jeremiah to intercede for this people (v. 11)! A wasted and fruitless prayer.

Hosea records the actual words of another prayer which seems to be filled with trust and confidence (Hos 6:1-3). Beginning with the recognition that the Lord is indeed able to heal the wounds resulting from their punishments (v. 1), the prayer expresses the conviction in faith that this same Lord will revive them after two days and raise them up on the third day "to live in his presence" (v. 2). The time reference suggests a short period, with deliverance relatively soon. The Christian community may have used the verse for explaining the Resurrection, but such was hardly intended by the words of the prayer as reported by Hosea. Since the Lord returns to the needs of his people like Spring rain each year, the people are confident that "as certain as the dawn is his coming" (v. 3). What initially seems like trust turns out to be arrogant presumption on cheap grace. What seems like faith is disclosed as an unwillingness to change. The divine response only underscores the fact that their piety is like "a morning cloud, like the dew that early passes away" (v. 4). Because their penance was without substance, the prophets were sent to slay the people with the harsh words of their lips. Only with genuine mercy (*hesed*) would God be pleased (v. 6)! Penance without mended community relationships was worthless in the eyes of Hosea. Regret without restitution or contrition without caring was useless.

Fortunately, Hosea also provides a prayer of sorrow which received the Lord's blessing and approval (14:2-4). The successful prayer which brought salvation and renewal gives us the opportunity to see which elements are uniquely present in contrast to those which only brought further rejection. This prayer is recorded as if the words are offered by the prophet himself and begins with a plea for forgiveness that the sacrifices might be acceptable (v. 3). Because Israel not only acknowledges that Assyria cannot save, but promises to cease treating human efforts as if they were God (v. 4), the prayer is successful. The Lord responds by putting his anger aside and becoming like dew for Israel (vv. 5-6). To treat any work of one's hands as if it were a supreme value in life, and to make any effort or possession the measurement for our existence is the fundamental idolatry renounced by this prayer. It is the

basic change which achieves forgiveness and renewed fruitfulness as a covenanted people.

Some prayers for salvation are successful. They are the
prayers which effect change in the human heart, not the
divine. Prophets offered salvation to those who recognized
that the covenant was conditional. If these texts are gleaned
from the public worship of Israel, and not merely from the
expressions of the inspired writer, they offer something for the
penance services and liturgical celebrations of all people who
would seek biblical patterns for modern needs. Shallow conversion remains the hazard of all religious traditions with
strong liturgical interests. The prophets were agents of change
who could always imagine a better, more just and more
humble manner of living as God's chosen people, without
arrogant dependence on their own efforts. It was inner change
they sought, not a quick shift in posture or a ready melody.

Pledges of Salvation

"My strength and my courage is the Lord, and he has been my
salvation (*yeshu'ah*). With joy you will draw water at the
fountain of salvation (*yesha'ah*)" (Is 12:2-3).

Sometimes as a result of events which brought deliverance
to the people of Israel, sometimes at the conclusion of rituals
which promised divine intervention, prophets felt summoned
to assure their audience of salvation. They raised their voices
in the midst of suffering and oppression in order to speak
clearly about the salvation which God inevitably brings to
faithful ones. In light of their prophetic gifts they were able to
see the signs of the beginning of that salvation which was still
hidden from the eyes of their contemporaries.

Once again an investigation into philology may provide insight into the splendid foundational reality so casually expressed by the word "salvation." The basic Hebrew word is *yasha'*, "to be broad, spacious or roomy." As a verb it is most commonly used in its causative (Hiphil) form, thus signifying the action of creating space or effectively providing an open area of safety for someone else. Perhaps only persons who have experienced the wide and seemingly endless expanses of the desert can truly understand the freedom of life which extends from horizon to horizon. Even the rolling wheat fields of midwestern United States cannot quite fill that bill because of the distraction of greenery which conspires to avoid the utter emptiness of the desert. Sarah and Abraham would have experienced the foundation of spacious salvation in a way which modern urban dwellers cannot.

Conversely, for Hebrews any trouble, pain or adversity is called a *sar*, literally "a tight spot," something narrow and confining from which one struggles for space, breath and freedom. The contemporary illustration which quickly comes to mind is the plight of little Jessica McClure, the little toddler from Texas who was suddenly wedged deep in an abandoned well in 1987, unable to extricate herself while the entire nation watched rescuers work frantically to reach her.

That event with its gripping drama gathers in itself all the fundamental issues inherent in the Hebrew notion of salvation and serves to illustrate the point vividly: a dynamic action of intervention in the face of great obstacles; in behalf of a person in serious trouble (from illness, judicial condemnation or any other danger); with little if any possibility of self-help; finally resulting in freedom and the opportunity to breathe, move and grow.

In the biblical tradition the concept was first invoked as a reference and explanation for narrow escape from Egypt. With the crack troops and chariots of the Pharaoh pressing against the backs of the fleeing Hebrews and water before them, suddenly at the last moment a path was opened and they fled through the Sea of Reeds to the freedom of the desert. In exultant celebration Miriam sang the words which proclaimed her faith, "My strength and my courage is the Lord, and he has been my salvation" (*yeshuah*; Ex 15:2). These words are almost exactly cited in the song of Isaiah quoted at the beginning of this section.

The stories of the judges returned to the same idea and experience of salvation. When the religious indifference of the Hebrews and their casual invocation of alien gods had repeatedly angered the Lord, he gave them into the hands of Mesopotamians and Moabites; but when they cried in their misfortune and servitude, that same God sent a savior (*moshia'*) to rescue and deliver them (Jgs 3:9, 15). These human instruments of salvation were weak human beings so that the Lord might be clearly seen as the real savior.

There is some evidence that the word savior (*moshia'*) was also a legal term, a title given to a person who came upon a situation of dire need or oppression and thus carried the obligation to intervene in behalf of the needy. In the law code of Deuteronomy, for example, a young woman sexually assaulted in the fields is presumed to have resisted, but because of the isolation did not have a savior (*moshia'*; Dt 22:27). Elsewhere those subject to the curses of the covenant were promised situations in which they would be blindly groping in darkness at noon, oppressed and without a savior (*moshia'*), or forced helplessly to watch their oxen slain before their eyes (29:31). In the villages of ancient Israel anyone who came upon the poor in need was expected to intervene energetically in their behalf, and thus become their savior. The concept and title was easily applied to God who had the obligation to step into history in order to free his people and give them space to breathe and grow.

The earliest classical prophets were consumed with the burden of announcing judgment upon their neighbors as a consequence of the injustice of that age. Neither Amos nor Hosea invoked the concept of salvation to any extent, even though the present form of those books ends on a more positive note.

Perhaps it was only with the scourge of the Assyrians toward the end of the eighth century B.C.E. that Isaiah began speaking of salvation with greater frequency. At that time the Assyrians moved through the land with mighty armies to besiege cities which elicited a fervent plea for deliverance from the people. He spoke of a "remnant" which would survive after the military ravages (Is 10:20-22; 11:16; 28:5). In modern usage the word remnant refers to a scrap of cloth, but it was a military term in ancient Israel, denoting the residue abandoned in the wake of a pillaging army. Small consolation perhaps, but a guarantee of survivors and safety for at least a few.

The song of Isaiah celebrated the confidence that was recommended to those who remained faithful, and described God as a never failing well whose waters are fresh and sweet. The refreshing delight of cool water in the heat of the day is the poetic image for escape from the burdens and oppression which only God can provide (12:3). Isaiah trusted in his God who always saves Israel from the tight spots of history, even those created by sin and malice. HIs contemporary, Micah, who lived in one of the towns near Jerusalem and experienced the same Assyrian fear, also expressed his confidence in his saving God, proudly stating, "My hope is in the God who saves me" (Mic 7:7).

The prophets were not only content to speak of salvation; they were themselves the signs and initial experiences of that reality. Isaiah gathered disciples and confided his teaching to them in anticipation of the day when freedom and space would again be given to Jerusalem (Is 8:16-18)! Jeremiah's escape from the dungeon in the house of Jonathan (Jer 37:15-21), and from Malchiah's cistern (38:6-13) was the first sign and pledge of the type of salvation which God would grant to all of Israel who remained faithful in oppression.

To speak of salvation in the age of the prophets or in our own day is to speak of the human condition at its deepest level of need. If things can be improved with a little more effort on the part of contemporary society, with more intelligent strategies or better distribution of monies, there would be no need for salvation. Those who are devoted to human progress as an inevitable process in history never speak of a savior in the biblical sense nor do they sense a need for one. Only those who experience and view the world as a problem radically incapable of solving itself or healing itself or moving itself into the wider spaces of freedom can look forward to salvation. Only then is there the opportunity for God to open a door which human beings cannot budge with their own effort.

This is particularly difficult for Americans to accept, for our nation is viewed as a land of "limitless opportunities" by those who sing its praises. It is a thoroughly middle class notion, not shared by those who struggle against the evils of racism, sexism or structural injustice. Those who are forced to live entrapped by ignorance or poverty seek a savior because they know they need one, while those who live as if everything is earned and deserved are the more to be pitied. Isaiah spoke harshly to those who lived by human agreement and manipulated treaties rather than by trust in a saving God (Is 30:1-3. 15).

The Day of the Lord

"Silence in the presence of the Lord God! For near is the day of the Lord" (Zeph 1:7).

In reading through the pages of inspired prophetic passages, we repeatedly come across references to the "Day of the Lord." In exploring the horizons of the harsh judgments pronounced by the prophets, we see that the phrase was readily available to them. Its origins are remote. It bears different tones, depending upon the context within which it is used.

Some see in the phrase "the Day of the Lord" a reference to the great interventions of Yahweh in the history of Israel's salvation. When Israel crossed the Red Sea in flight from the Pharaoh's chariots, they were told to be still, for their Lord would fight in their behalf (Ex 14:14). The victory was an occasion for annual celebration among all succeeding generations. The book of Judges recounts time after time when the Lord's anger flared up against his people for their idolatry and allowed them to fall into the hands of hostile neighbors (Jgs 2:13-19). Whenever they cried out, the Lord raised up a savior again to deliver them. The military exploits of their champion who called them to faith as well as to victorious strategy marked Days of the Lord. Sometimes the Israelites quarreled and tested God's presence in their midst, as at Massah and Meribah (Ex 17:1-7), but even then the Lord intervened for their safety and deliverance. If such be the origin of the phrase, the plea for the Day of the Lord is a prayer for divine intervention similar to the great events of the past, with military action and faith. The context would be the "Holy War," but projected on a vast world-wide scale. The more difficult the situation, and the more ardent the prayer, the more the "Day of the Lord" was viewed as a final and definitive redemption by the Lord. His faithful would be supreme and could exercise vengance against all their political enemies!

For others the notion is more properly rooted in the liturgy of the Temple in Jerusalem. Some psalms seem to exhibit a common pattern of rebellion and divine victory. Psalm 2, for example, celebrates the raging of the nations and the conspiracy of foreign princes against the Lord and his anointed (vv. 1-2). The issue was rebellion against the sovereign power of the Lord. It probably provided a generic profile which could fit the specific foe of any given age. God's response is first one of derision, for human rebellion is empty and futile (v. 4), but it quickly became anger and reaffirmation of the divine authority of the king on Mount Zion (vv. 5-6) to whom the ends of the earth had been given. The psalm concuded with the promise of an iron rod for ruling the nations (v. 9) and an invitation to humble faithful service lest the same treatment be given to rebellious citizens in Jerusalem.

Psalm 93 offers a similar set of elements, but fixes the rebellion in the surging waves of mythical antiquity rather than in the real nations who happened to become feisty at the time. Beginning with a magnificent liturgical confession of the majesty of Yahweh, robed in splendor and strength (v. 1), it moves to acknowledge the surging of the waves against his eternal throne (v. 3). Since the Lord is more powerful than the roar of many waters, the Temple of the Lord is filled with holiness and power (vv. 4-5). Water was the symbol of evil, power and death, and the raging waves of the Mediterranean or Sea of Galilee easily became the sign of rebellion. In crossing over the Red Sea or the Jordan, the Lord had demonstrated his power over all evil forces in creation. Some scholars would presume the existence of a dramatic liturgy in Jerusalem, possibly dating from pre-Hebrew Jebusite days, when the stability of Zion would be celebrated as the annual "Day of the Lord." This explanation would bring a strong liturgical note to the concept, and a conviction that any human foe was merely the temporary expression of a deeper rebellion against the Lord. The powers of evil were controlled in this explanation by the ritual enactment of God's victory. Since the word was powerful and effective, the mere recitation of the ancient story of the raging waves was able to bring peace and tranquility to the land again.

In either case, when Amos uttered his famous "Woe to those who yearn for the day of the Lord" (Am 5:18), he clearly referred to the popular expectation of imminent deliverance from the military advances of the Assyrian army. It was a century which was witnessing the resurgence of that great terror, and the affluence of Samaria was an attractive object for conquest. To those who thronged to the shrine at Bethel, pleading for a new "Day of the Lord" in which evil would be contained and defeated, Amos had startling words indeed. What was viewed as a sign of salvation and a promise of divine intervention became a mixed metaphor on the lips of Amos. It would indeed be salvation, but only to those who remained profoundly faithful to the spirit of the covenant! To others it would be a day of darkness, not light (v. 18). It would bring the terrible surprise experienced by one who rushed into a home for safety only to find that a serpent would bite his hand as he rested breathlessly leaning against the wall (v. 19). It was salvation for the poor and oppressed alone.

Without using the actual phrase, Nahum invokes all the terminology of the "Day of the Lord" in his celebration of the moral victory of the Lord over the evil of Nineveh. The Lord is good, "a refuge on the day of distress" taking care of those who have recourse to him (Hab 1:7). It was surely an oracle of salvation for those who longed for divine reversal of power toward justice and peace. Although Zephaniah also came before the final destruction of Nineveh, as evident from the prophet's promise that God would destroy Assyria (Zeph 2:13), he seems to turn his attention to the local religious corruption. Those in Jerusalem itself who indulged in the practices of the foreign nations were the objects of the destruction expected in the Day of the Lord. Almost like the slaughter of a great victim for sacrifice, the Lord was described as purifying all his invited guests in preparation for the event. With language reminiscent of liturgy, Zephaniah speaks of a day when the earth will be swept clean of all wicked creatures (1:3). Even the names of those priests who dared to serve Baal would be wiped away forever (v. 4) together with all who have "fallen away from the Lord" (v. 6). With magnificent imagery Zephaniah splashes a massive mural of the final bitter attack of the Lord against the rich, the powerful and the famous who represent the evil of his age. Although some verses clearly promise the end of all who live on earth (v. 18), Zephaniah is quick to clarify that the "humble of the earth" (2:3) to whom the speech is directed will be saved! It is an oracle of salvation and reminds the poor and lowly of the fact that the Lord is in their midst, and will rejoice with them "as one sings at festivals" (3:17-18) without disgrace.

The book of Ezekiel also contains a section which seems to reflect the pattern of the "Day of the Lord" as well. In the prophecies against Gog and Magog (Ez 38-39), we read of great armies being stirred up against Israel to prove the salvific power and holiness of the Lord (38:14-16). These mighty nations, marching out in power, would suddenly be struck down forever. So complete is the destruction that it will take seven months merely to bury the dead (39:12)! The moral and physical sovereignty of the Lord and the final salvation of his people is the truth proclaimed by this prophetic theme.

The entire theme contains a warning for those who ardently pray for their nation's success and victory over the enemy of the day. Ancient or modern, the oracles warn that one should be very careful lest he or she be surprised at the end to discover that the victory comes against rather than for their side!

The Anointed One to Come

"For a child is born to us, a son is given to us; upon his shoulder dominion rests. They name him Wonderful-Counselor, God-Hero, Father-Forever, Prince of Peace" (Is 9:5).

Christian readers of the prophetic scriptures may be surprised to learn that there were many anointed figures in Israel, and the special focus of our faith convictions finds far less explicit preparation than we might expect. It was primarily kings who were anointed in Israel, sometimes in secrecy as when Samuel anointed Saul or David, sometimes in full view of the nation as when Solomon was proclaimed King in Jerusalem. This anointing was a ritual symbol of the gift of the Spirit for leadership. Strength, healing, beauty and lavish perfumed respect were explanations for the anointing. Prophets gave oracles stating the wondrous results of the new king's rule. The king became a special son of the Lord in covenant. "I shall be a father to him and he shall be a son to me" (2 Sam 7:14) were the words spoken by Nathan of Solomon. Psalm 110 may represent something of a coronation rite, with the oracle "Before the daystar, like the dew, I have begotten you"

(Ps 110:3) addressed to the new king. They ruled over enemies and became an instrument for the Lord's vanquishing of foreign rebellious kings.

The promise to David included that a successor would always be present as a sign of the Lord's care and protection for his people. Experience demonstrated that these rulers were not always faithful to the image nor to the expectations of their people. Often injustice, avarice and idolatry marked their successive rules, and devious treaties with Egypt or Assyria to obtain easy protection in one tough spot or another. The anointed human king as an instrument of salvation was ambivalent. Each time a new king came upon the scene, the people gathered again to hope that he would be filled with wise counsel, military strength of a champion, fatherly care as if for widows and orphans and the fullness of peace. Titles were given and throne names such as those in the oracle for Hezekiah cited from the installation oracle of Isaiah (Is 9:2-6).

Only as the situation became more desperate did the people begin to seek an Anointed who would come to set things straight once and for all.[1] Only long after the pages of the Hebrew Scriptures had been finished did the people look forward to the end of historical ages in successions of peaks and valleys, and seek the Anointed Such is beyond the pre-exilic dreams of the prophets. They did make a contribution to the salvation of their people by recognizing that some are indeed called to be instruments of God's deliverance, but only those who are humble and faithful. The rest are swept away in the Day of the Lord. Those who see penance as only for the other person are themselves rejected as unfit for

---

[1]The classic study in the biblical development of this concept is S. Mowinckel, *He That Cometh* (Abingdon, 1954).

the salvation which only the Lord can promise and deliver. Only the humble and faithful are allowed to return home from the exile of their hearts where selfishness once reigned.

꙳

Three measuring sticks for those who seek to share the salvation promised by the prophets:

Which type of return from Exile remains close to your heart today?

How can the nation experience the type of penance demanded by the prophets in their rituals for conversion?

If the Anointed-yet-to-Come has communal dimensions, how do his characteristics measure up against the spirit of the faith-community today?

8

Images for God

First and foremost prophets are people who see more clearly than most folks of their age, and they are messengers who simply cannot refrain from speaking about the world they have come to know from the inside. Prophets inevitably make connections between the world of human behavior and the less human (but sometimes more humane) creatures of the world. They are keenly aware of the moral dimensions of life. They see similarities and patterns of behavior and make surprising comparisons. They are often poets of remarkable skill and sensitivity.

It should not be surprising that such individuals would use fresh and striking images to describe and communicate the reality they saw breaking into the arena of history and politics. Before the abundance of written records, the spoken word was the guardian of social custom and responsibility. It was seen as powerful and effective. Sometimes it was remembered because it repeated familiar phrases long sanctified by usage for a particular purpose. Literary forms helped to keep things clear in the give and take of daily life. On other occasions the speech was remembered because it included an expression so novel that it captivated the audience with its clarity and keen insight. The friend and disciple or enemy and rival remembered the prophet's words with precision. Perhaps an adage was born or a fresh manner of describing the work of God. Sometimes collections of prophetic speeches were peppered with delightful images or gathered around the nucleus of a remarkably deft turn of phrase or spiritual insight.

Examples of the poetic skill of pre-exilic prophets are virtually endless. Amos could allude to the mountains melting away at the touch of God's hot angry feet (Am 9:5), and Hosea could portray the Lord as gathering thorn-branches and brambles to form the edges of a path from which Israel could not escape (Hos 2:8). Isaiah saw that human guilt could suddenly erupt into disaster and compared it to a crack which rips through a wall and occasions an instantaneous collapse in an earthquake, or a jar which slips from one's hand to shatter across the ground in tiny fragments (Is 30:13-14). Jeremiah is rightfully famous for observing that a leopard could as easily change its spots as his neighbors begin acting decently (Jer 14:23).

Among all the imagery, we meet some very striking characteristics attributed to God. Descriptions are cast around the Lord's neck like ornaments and God arrives on the stage of Israel's history in a thousand roles. Sometimes the masks are frightening and serve to make Israel and any modern reader think twice; sometimes they are very consoling and comforting. They describe some very different facets of the God of Israel. An exploration into the poetic imagery of the prophets represents an excellent starting point for personal prayer.

Images Of Terror

"The glory of Ephraim flies away like a bird: no birth, no

carrying in the womb, no conception. Were they to bear children, I would slay the darlings of their womb" (Hos 9:11).

To speak of the Lord as a baby-killer is a harsh and dreadful thing! Yet this is precisely what Hosea did to express the deadly anger of the Lord of Life. If children were viewed as a blessing, then barrenness was a curse and the death of children at the hands of a foreign nation acting with divine permission, a terrible tragedy. Many diverse actions are attributed to the Lord, each perhaps triggered by the realization that God was named as a verb. Punishment was always intended to prepare for eventual blessing. We explore some of the negative images in order to appreciate the forcefulness with which the prophets addressed their messages to their age and ours.

When Amos announced the series of punishments about to fall upon the neighboring nations of Israel, he repeatedly spoke of the Lord "sending fire" upon their walls (Am 1:7. 10. 12). The verb is an intensive form which suggests being released into freedom, or being sent forth with deliberation and finality. The same form was used when Moses confronted the Pharaoh, demanding "Let my people go" (Ex 5 1) or when a man was forbidden to divorce (literally send away) his wife unjustly (Dt 22:19). In fact the technical word for divorce is the same intensive form of "sending." The image used by Amos paints the Lord as releasing a personified servant-like fire to rush out and destroy the city walls of nations which violate covenants. This would in turn leave them vulnerable to attack and devastation. Hosea uses the very same image (Hos 8:14).

Isaiah goes on to speak of the Light of Israel turned into a conflagration, consuming Israel like so many briers and brambles (Is 10:17), or a gigantic bonfire, piled high with grass and dry wood, kindled with brimstone/sulphur and the hot breath of God against Assyria (Is 30:33). Jeremiah speaks of poisonous snakes being "sent" in the same fashion against Israel, but without any charm for healing (Jer 8:17). All of creation stands at the bid of the Lord.

Lion

One of the most popular and powerful images of terror in ancient Israel or Judah was the lion. Some species of large feline roamed the banks of the Jordan and terrorized the inhabitants of the land during the days of the prophets. It provided a ready image for the punishing action of the Lord, quick and deadly in its power. Sharing the rage of his God in the face of injustice, Amos begins by describing the Lord as "roaring from Zion" (Am 1:2). He reverts back to the lion image to explain God's actions, for the lion only roars when it has prey in its paw (3:4) and creates an immediate and instinctive fear in those who hear, similar to the spontaneous speech of the prophet who hears the Lord (3:8).

Hosea makes the identification more direct, for he quotes the Lord as growling, "I am like a lion (*shahal*) to Ephraim, like a young lion (*kephir*) to the house of Judah; it is I who rend the prey and depart, I carry it away and no one can save it from me" (Hos 5:14).The word used for lion imitates the low reverberating growl which fills the lungs of an angry beast protecting its catch. The Hebrew word for young lion refers to a near adult, first covered with its shaggy mane and swaggering in its initial prowess. Thus the Lord growls at anyone who would attempt to rescue Ephraim from his teeth; he rips apart Judah, mauling it and resolutely carrying it away. Hosea uses yet a third word to describe the Lord who "roars like a lion (*'aryeh*)" so that the exiled people of Ephraim will come creeping back in fright from Egypt (11 10). This final Hebrew term highlights the beast as capable of ripping and tearing the flesh of all who resist or put up a fight. Finally, Hosea returns to the image in describing the punishment allotted to those who eat their fill and forget the God who fed them in the desert. To them he will be "like a lion (*shahal*) to them, like a panther by the road" (13:7), or "like a bear robbed of its young" (v. 8), tearing their hearts from their breasts and devouring them on the spot!

Isaiah also invokes the image of the mauling lion and scruffy shaggy young adult which refuses to abandon its prey, no matter how much noise the assembled band of shepherds might make (Is 31:4). From every aspect the image is very apt, underscoring the power, agility, and anger of a God determined to punish. From the terror of an angry God, there is no escape. Micah thinks the ragged and beaten remnant of Judah at Bethlehem could also become a lion in the midst of the nations (Mic 5:7), showing that the same imagery can be used for a blessing too!

Moth and Maggot

Hosea's poetic imagination is hardly exhausted by his reflections on the lion lurking in the brush. He also noted that Ephraim had "willingly gone after filth" (Hos 5:11), then quickly leapt in mental logic to quote the Lord as announcing "I am like a moth (*'ash*) for Ephraim, like maggots (*raqab*) for the house of Judah" (v. 12). The Hebrew word for moth suggests an inner destruction which results in the ragged and tattered, weak and utterly useless condition of the item so afflicted. The word translated as "maggots" in the New American Bible more properly refers to the rottenness and decay which destroys wood, leaving it crumbled and useless. When the same condition afflicts flesh, the maggots congregate. Those who seek filth, says Hosea, become rotten themselves, and God is the gnawing devastation from within. Given Hosea's preoccupation with fertility cults and sexuality, a later translator might suggest some form of venereal disease as the punishment, and imply that the Lord is the ultimate agent. Poets leap from immediate to ultimate causes quickly, and Hebrew prophets ascribed everything eventually to God alone.

Punishing Visitor

The pre-exilic prophets repeatedly describe the Lord as "punishing" Israel or Judah, and in the context of so much heaped up judgment, the word becomes rather bland. In fact the word itself has a special nuance because *paqad* means to "appear on the scene" or to "visit." It could mean to "strike, search, punish" if the visit is negative and punitive. Amos invokes the image of such a visit precisely because Israel was known and favored above all the nations of the earth (Am 3:2), and the same type of "visit" will be experienced by the altars of Bethel where the Lord was usually anticipated as present to bless with prosperity and beneficence (v. 14). In reviewing these passages, the modern reader should be acutely conscious of the fact that all passive verbs are presumed to have the Lord as the agent. Respect for the Divine Name led prophets and editors to express divine action in the passive, but the forceful effect was understood as anything but passive!

Hosea speaks of the Lord bringing the blood of the slaughtered house of Jezreel to visit General Jehu (Hos 1:4). It is an unexpected punishment for someone initially commissioned by Elisha (2 K 9:1-15), but ruthlessly bloody in eliminating the entire family of Ahab (10:1-11). When the children's heads arrive in a basket, it was like the bloody coup of a South American dictator, perhaps begun in the name of justice, but becoming equally unjust and bloody. In the eyes of the prophets, no commission, howsoever urgent and sacred, is free from eventual accountability. In Hosea's poetry, the blood itself comes back for a surprise visit. The Lord also visits Israel as she burns incense to Baal (Hos 2:15). God likewise visits priests as they feed on the guilt of their congregation (4:9; 8:13).

Isaiah speaks of sudden visits from the Lord, surrounded by thunder, earthquake, whirlwind, storm and fire (Is 29:6), and Zephaniah laments that these "visits" have proven fruitless for Jerusalem (Zeph 3:7). In all these instances, it is the sudden arrival of the superior or supervisor which causes panic and on occasions punishment. Early Christian parables which warn of the sudden return of the master draw upon this prophetic theme (Lk 12:35-40).

Crowds of other images appear helter-skelter in the poetic threats of the prophets. Amos can conjure up the portrait of a God sending a personified famine to visit the northern kingdom of Israel (Am 8:11) and actually picking clean the very teeth of the people so that they are desperately hungry, not for bread, but for the nourishment of the Word of God (4:6). It is after all not by bread alone that people subsist (Dt 8:3). Those who flee from the judgment of God cannot escape, for the Lord will "hunt them out" (literally dig them out of the earth and pry them loose from the rocks under the soil) no matter how hard they attempt escape (Am9:3). It is the same Lord who will crush others into the ground, like a wagon pressed down into the sandy soil by an impossible load, and preventing even the swift, trained runners from speedy exit (2:13). Into the quicksand or mire they go, immobile until caught by the fruits of their crimes.

When Amos details the accusations against Israel, he rehearses the elements of a lawsuit against the people associated with worship at Bethel (Am 2:6-16). Hosea is more explicit in describing the legal grievance of the Lord against the inhabitants of the land (Hos 4:1) and the priests (v. 4), or the controversy initiated by God over the way Israel was trafficking in deceit and sending oil off to Egypt (12:2-3). God is imaged as Plaintiff, prosecuting Attorney and Judge in the case. Justice would be done, and Isaiah even describes the Lord rising in court to present his case (Is 3:13), or stand as Witness (Zeph 1:2; 3:8).

Like a tight-lipped determined Farmer, the Lord was pictured as doggedly trying to yoke and train a stubborn heifer which resisted the task of plowing (Hos 10:11). Like a Meteorologist on the evening news, the Lord is depicted as announcing and summoning the burning east wind (13:15; see Jer 18:17). The Lord is even called a whirling storm of devastating proportions (Jer 23:19). The tornadoes of Kansas or the hurricanes of the Caribbean provide some more graphic dimensions for the reality so described by Jeremiah.

Like a Hunter, the Lord spread a net to capture the silly and senseless dove, Ephraim (Hos 7:12), and Isaiah actually calls God a "snare" (*pah*), stretched out to entangle feet in the twigs and branches (Is 8:14). The same God is able to whistle for the beasts of Assyria to come like hunting dogs (5:26) or bees and flies to torment Judah (7:18-19).

Like a grim Warrior engaged in a ritual sanctified by its strategic intent, the Lord strikes with pestilence (Am 4:9-10) and sword (9:1), which were venerated as demi-gods in ancient Ugarit. He snaps their weapons (Hos 1:5), no matter how advanced and lethal, and gathers armies at his word (8:10). He barks out orders and strengthens the arms of his soldiers with training calisthenics (Is 7:15). He humiliates captives by shaving their bodies (7:20) and sending them naked off to exile where they will die of hunger (5:13). Relentlessly cruel is this portrait, and Habakkuk refines the picture even further by heaping up a collage of allusions to ready arrows in the quiver, flashing spear and burnished shafts (Hab 3:9-14).

Amos describes Yahweh as forming little locusts out of clay to punish Israel (Am 7:1). Isaiah speaks of the same Lord crowning the beautiful women of Jerusalem with baldness and scabs (Is 3:17) or casting the deep sleep (*tardemah*) which accompanied the creation of Eve (Gen 2:21) upon the rulers of Jerusalem (29:10) so they would not perform their duties. Micah imagined the Lord shoving statues and buildings down the ravine into the valley below the city of Samaria, destroying the capital city piece by piece (Mic 1 6).

One after the other, the prophets pluck images of terror from the world around them to illustrate the seriousness of their message. A modern urban age might use the vicious mugging heroin addict in the alley by night in place of the lion, or the lethal destruction of nuclear waste rather than the moth, but the effect of each image remains the same. So does the threat implied therein.

Sketches of Blessing

"On that day the Lord of hosts will be a glorious crown and a brilliant diadem to the remnant of his people" (Is 28:5).

Obviously not all the imagery invoked by the pre-exilic prophets was negative, even though the threat of punishment remained the major portion and burden of their messages. Punishment came over the horizon in order to refine and purify, to discipline and convert. Except for the historical person of Amos himself who seemed unable to imagine anything beyond the terrible destruction he envisioned, the others described the blessings of a saving God as well when they placed the fundamental choices before their contemporaries.

If Hosea imagined the Lord stripping Israel naked for her public shame (Hos 2:5), it was in order to once again become her divine Fiancee (vv. 21-22) and to provoke her wholehearted response to God's blandishments (vv. 17, 23-24). Almost as if with a kiss, God would remove the very name of Baal from her mouth (v. 19). Hosea shifted back and forth in the gender of his imagery as he attempted to paint the possibility of a daring yet enticing future, attributing to Yahweh a visceral womb-like affection and pity for Judah, almost like a mother for a favored daughter (1:7). The same God was a proud father, teaching his infant to walk and tenderly healing the child's baby bruises (11:1-3). The covenantal implications of the latter image have been briefly explored elsewhere. Hosea seems to have influenced Jeremiah in many areas of thought, for Jeremiah also speaks of Yahweh as master/husband (*baal*; Jer 3:14 and 31:32) and father (3:19).

Although in one context Hosea might deny the possibility of a savior to Israel (13:4), a contrary vein of mercy prevailed in the work as it stands, and salvation is ultimately promised, "but not by war" (1:7). Not surprisingly, Isaiah celebrates the Lord as Savior (Is 12:2) since the prophet's personal name acknowledged that reality. The two words stemmed from the same Hebrew root. Jeremiah also wove the image of savior into his poetry, especially for those in need (Jer 14:8), but placed it in the midst of an unacceptable prayer of contrition. The Hebrew verb *yasha'* means to "be spacious," and then "to be freed, saved, delivered" as contrasted with danger, which is usually associated with a tight spot. Some would suggest that the person first titled savior in the social life of the Hebrews was the one who intervened in legal proceedings to free captives or those under the shadow of punishment. If the origin is correct, the concept would carry with it the suggestion of freeing from institutional harassment and social strictures.

Isaiah's poetic forays were not limited to occupational allusions in his attempt to describe the Lord. In the text used above to introduce this section, he calls God a crown (*'ateret*) and diadem (*sephirah*) for the remnant of his people (Is 28:5). The former suggested a circular ornament denoting honor and special dignity, and the latter a circle of dancers and sign of festive celebration. For Isaiah the Lord is the cap of honor and the badge of authority at a royal coronation or Mardi Gras celebration, a mark of distinction and public recognition. The crown of the Miss America Pageant or an Olympic gold medal is about as close as our democratic society can come to Isaiah's imagery for God in this instance.

On occasion images of terror are transformed into signs and sketches of hope, for the military Lord can be a champion and mighty warrior for salvation (Zeph 3:17). The sudden visitation can be for restoration (2:7), especially in behalf of the humble and lowly remnant who have remained faithful.

Isaiah walked through the busy streets of Jerusalem and associated many trades and occupations with the work of the

Lord who became at times like the smelter and refiner of precious metals, burning off the dross and refuse from the molten silver of Jerusalem (Is 1:25). In another context God was presented as the Owner of an exquisite vineyard, well manicured and carefully kept, which produced nothing but sour wild grapes (5:1-6; see Jer 1:21). One can almost hear the boasting of successful farmers or their complaints over profitless harvests between the lines of Isaiah's song.

On still another occasion Isaiah painted the Lord's portrait as a teacher, probably modeled after the image of those members of the royal court or heads of noble academies in Jerusalem, patiently instructing children in the graces of life and the values of learning (2:3-4; 3:20; see Mic 4:2). Those who dealt with wisdom and the proverbs of the nation seem to have had considerable influence upon the thought and words of Isaiah. The prophet himself may even have been an instructor or tenured professor in his day as evidenced by his reflections on the mysteries of planting and harvesting (Is 28:23-29). Those who contributed to the collections of proverbs demonstrated a great deal of knowledge of the natural world of creation around them.

The passage is similar to the many agricultural observations of Proverbs. Isaiah clearly pondered the things he witnessed in the course of his daily walks through the city or countryside! Commentators have suggested that the portrait of the ideal wife (Prov 31:10-31) represents an advertisement for the graceful young women who might be enrolled in one of these academies in Jerusalem. Isaiah saw any number of occupations and projected them upon the work of the Lord like a poetic overlay.

The uncontroverted authentic texts of Isaiah himself seem hesitant to ascribe the image of King to the Lord, even though the psalms were familiar with such a usage. Zephaniah found it attractive and hopeful (Zeph 3:15), as did Jeremiah who even extended the Lord's rule to the nations/*goim* (Jer 10:7-10).

A lengthy litany of other colorful images attempt to sketch the good and gracious God in the midst of a converted and purified Israel and Judah. The Lord could be compared to the shining light of dawn (Hos 6:3) even if the context is once more an unacceptable prayer of repentance. The Lord is a profound healing (14:4) and life-giving dew (v. 5) which sustains plants and people during the dry season in Judah each year. For Isaiah, one might describe God as an eye-catching banner (*nes*), almost miraculous in its ability to gather outcasts and bring them home (Is 11:12). The reference reminds us of the poles used by guides to unite weary tourists and bring them safely and quickly through crowded museums toward home. The same prophet likens God to a canopy for protection in heat or storm (4:6) or even to a flock of birds hovering over Jerusalem to protect the inhabitants by warning of sudden danger from newcomers (31:5). Micah speaks of gathering the lame and outcasts like a shepherd herds his flock into the corral (Mic 2:12; 4:6) and of the Lord as a guiding light in the darkness of a society without electricity (7:8).

Although the Yahwist described the Lord as the potter of the universe, especially in reference to the earthling Adam (Gen 2:7), and although Amos applied the same to the plague of locusts (Am 7:1), Jeremiah made his own contribution to the literary heritage of Judah and Israel, speaking of the Lord as the potter who molds and fashions the clay of all things (Jer 10:16). Any reference to "creator" in Scripture should carry with it the overtones of hands deep into the clay of things, shaping their inner being for some purpose with artistry and skill. Jeremiah also launches into new territory when he pictures the Lord as a "searcher (*bohen*) of mind (literally 'kidneys') and heart" (11:20) or one who alone can "probe (*hoqer*) the mind (literally 'kidneys') and test (*bohen*) the heart" (17:10; see 20:12). This image was a brilliant essay into the mystery of God who is likened to one who rubs metal, testing for value (*bahan*), or to a miner who digs into the earth, searching out its buried secrets (*haqar*). In the primitive physiology of Hebrew culture, the heart was the place of decision and planning, not sentimental love as in modern cultures, and the kidneys were the locations of the conscience. Jeremiah had no secrets from this persistent divine therapist who dug into his very being like an eager prospector for gold or an examiner of fine antiques. For Jeremiah, the Lord was a persistent gardener, weeding out evil neighbors from their land like dandelions (12:14), acting like a strong rock of refuge to those in need (16:19) or a mighty rock-shattering hammer to those who resisted his will (23:29)! He was a mighty champion for his people, a Goliath in their defense (20:11). Zephaniah transformed that warrior into the host of an immense banquet, with ritual victims slaughtered for all the invited guests (Zeph 1:7).

The words and images may limp at times, as all human poetry must when projected against the divine. Each image was measured against what the community knew to be true of the Lord. Those which rendered the Lord concretely present and graphically active were retained eagerly. The very fact that the community subsequently canonized these bits of poetic intuition and insight is an encouragement to take the same process to prayer and reclothe the same insights in modern garb.

❧

Three sparks for a modern poetic imagination:

What images might one choose from contemporary society or newspaper headlines to describe the destructive and terrible punishment promised to those who treat God cavalierly today?

What images might one glean from catalogues or advertisements to image the blessings given to those who humbly await the vindication of their lives and the success of their causes?

Which prophetic image for God is your favorite and how does it sustain you in the ambiguities or injustices of life?

9

Further Thoughts From The Community Of Faith

The various messages and pronouncements of the pre-exilic prophets were gathered by disciples of one sort or another. Shorter collections came into being and were treasured in circles of religious personnel. Priests at a shrine preserved some; relatives or neighbors may have been instrumental in conserving others. Each new recitation or reading disclosed more profound meaning and insight in the words and images. Those prophets whose words had been vindicated by history were revered as truly sent by God and monuments to their name were built among the tombs of the Kedron Valley. In the hindsight of history, their prophetic message had proven too important to forget. They were perceived as perennially valuable. The same patterns of human selfishness, rebellion, indifference and injustice were engraved on the human heart everywhere and all could profit from the Word of God.

The role of the community in preserving these prophetic messages may never be minimized. It was the faith of each generation which sifted and tested the messages claimed to have been received from divine inspiration. It was the religious leaders who preserved for posterity the best from the words and lives of the early prophets.

With each new recitation, fresh applications of the same message were discovered. Sin and salvation became patterns which fitted every location and generation. The fundamental insight of each individual prophet came to be the measure of each successive age: the justice of Amos, the fidelity of Hosea, the trust of Isaiah, the repentance of Jeremiah and the glorious ritual purity of Ezekiel. The God who had brought Israel out of slavery in Egypt (Am 2:10; Mic 6:4; Jer 1:6) disclosed one type of bondage after another.

And Then There was Judah

"Thus says the Lord: 'For three crimes of Judah, and for four, I will not revoke my word'" (Am 2:4)

After the northern kingdom of Israel had gone into exile at the hand of the Assyrians in 721 B.C.E., the Deuteronomic historians and theologians came south to Judah. They were welcomed by the saintly Hezekiah and their words heeded by the equally saintly Josiah a century later. These kings of Judah listened to the Deuteronomic explanation for the fall of the north and determined to avoid a similar fate at the hands of foreign gods and tyrants. The situation might be somewhat similar to those who had witnessed the inner decay of Nazi Germany in our century, now citing evidence for the same disease in other lands.

Those who had collected the searing warnings of prophets in Israel now began to shape their messages in such a way that they would speak to the people of Judah as well. An introduction to each prophetic collection was added with explicit references to their contemporary kings in Judah as well as in Israel (Am 1:1; Hos 1:1).Both nations shared common traditions in faith and both stood under similar judgment as covenanted peoples. The word had been uttered at a given moment in history, and the times were not all that different, at least not in the eyes of those who read the prophetic oracles from the vantage point of life in Jerusalem.

To the litany of nations judged by Amos at Bethel was newly added an indictment of Judah (Am 2:4-5). The crimes were phrased in language quite unique in the book of Amos and spoke in very general terms about spurning Torah and Yahweh's covenant stipulations. It was clearly an addition for the sake of *aggiornamento,* coming from lips (or pens) other than those of Amos. The message was the same, but the target had become more inclusive. The purpose was to make sure that Judah didn't affirm the punishment of Israel too blithely. After all, it became increasingly clear that the southern kingdom was guilty of the same crimes.

When Hosea directed his words to his erring northern neighbors, his entire focus was probably upon the people of Israel alone. As the work was shaped into its definitive form, references to Judah were added under the inspiration of the prophetic spirit. In contrast to Israel, an expression of pity for Judah was added, and a promise of salvation, but not by the efforts of the military establishment (Hos 1:7)! Hope was expressed that Judah not be guilty of the spiritual prostitution enjoyed in Israel (4:15). A marginal notation was appended to a description of the stumbling of Ephraim, to the effect that Judah stumbled right along (5:5). "Walking" was the short-hand image for moral behavior, and prophets began to notice how badly Judah was limping those days. If Ephraim was denounced for groveling before the great king of Assyria, searching for weapons and protection, so did Judah (v. 13). If Hosea had cried in anguish over his inability to handle

Ephraim, someone then added, "What can I do with you, Judah?" (6:4). The circle of crime and anguish was spreading, and the appropriate harvest was appointed for Judah too (v. 11)! The punishment announced by a later editor of Amos was also directed at Judah and fire was unleashed against the cities to the south (8:14).

The stern warnings of Isaiah were aimed at the southern kingdom where the prophet lived. He described Zion as a blighted and drought-stricken tree with falling leaves (Is 1:30) and as a flimsy shed in a melon patch (v. 8). Turning toward the north, Isaiah promised a return to those pitifully few survivors of the earlier Assyrian exile (10:20-21). A century later Jeremiah would offer similar hope for Rachel's lost northern children (Jer 31:15-16). Both promises stayed in place after Judah's eventual exile and became words of hope for Judah as well. Just as a certain *aggiornamento* had been achieved by including Judah along with guilty Israel, so another later *aggiornamento* was accomplished by including Judah in the promise of return from exile. Before that could happen, the destruction of Jerusalem had to be accomplished. Micah's promise that Zion would be a plowed field and Jerusalem a heap of stones (Mic 3:12) became a dreadful reality. The phrase was remembered when Jeremiah came to say the same thing (Jer 26:16-19) and temporarily got him off the hook of capital punishment, for Hezekiah had not stricken Micah for such dire pronouncements!

Nahum was so distracted by his hatred for Nineveh, that he could be totally oblivious to the relatively minor peccadillos of Judah. "Celebrate your feast, O Judah, fulfill your vows! For nevermore shall you be invaded by the scoundrel" (Nah 2:1). He was correct, of course, for it would be Babylon, not Assyria, whom the Lord would unleash upon Zion.

Jeremiah and Zephaniah directed virtually all their prophetic lives and words toward Jerusalem. The last verse of Zephaniah ends the brief book on a note of hope for the exiles of Judah, promising that the Lord would gather them and bring them home, giving them praise and renown among all the nations (Zeph 3:20). It must have stemmed from a later age after the capture of Jerusalem by the Babylonians (Chaldeans) in 587 B.C.E. Sin, warning, continued sin, exile and return formed the major elements in the mosaic. The entire pattern for the experience of Israel was stretched to fit Judah as well. Later disciples and members of prophetic schools made those little adjustments in text and tone to assure the perennial validity of the words of God's prophets.

Pastoral Postscripts

"Let whoever is wise understand these things; let whoever is prudent know them. Straight are the paths of the Lord, in them the just (*sedaqim*) walk, but sinners stumble in them" (Hos 14:10).

Gradually listeners became readers as the speeches of prophets were recorded for posterity and read aloud by subsequent generations. The exact period of the codification of the prophetic canon did not occur until the fourth century B.C.E. in all probability. The establishment of the synagogue as a place of study and worship may have been even later although some would seek to situate the origin of the synagogue in the Babylonian exile (roughly 587-537 B.C.E.). They gathered in small places of assembly for prayer and study for they instinctively knew that the Word of God was intended to be a social experience, not limited to the heart of a solitary listener.

The faith of those who collected the prophetic words could not abide a threat of punishment as the last word of Yahweh in any literary work of a religious nature. Therefore, they added oracles of hope and salvation at the end of each collection. Even Amos received a glowing epilogue which muted the dire portrait of the earlier nine chapters. All the total destruction was recast as a sifting for pebbles of value (Am 9:9). The fallen hut of the house of David, which had completely disappeared by the time of the final editing, was promised a rebuilding "as in the days of old" (v. 11). All the old curses of Deuteronomy, namely such frustrations as "building a house, but not living in it" or "planting a vineyard, but not enjoying its fruits" (Dt 28:30-34), are reversed in the final note to Amos. Those same curses were part of the threat of Micah: sowing without reaping, eating without being satisfied, and desperately acquiring without saving (Mic 6:14-15; see Hag 1:6). The pastoral editors of Amos simply could not allow such threats to be the final state because that was not the God they worshipped. Moreover, by that time history had already witnessed some limited form of restoration. Consequently, the final editors concluded the text with a portrait of an agricultural effort so prosperous that the harvesters would still be gathering in the Autumn produce when the Spring sowers came to work the following year (Am 9:13-14)! The end time couldn't be any different if the Lord of salvation were really in charge.

Similarly Hosea's words end with a promise that Israel would eventually become fragrant like a lily, splendid like an olive and fragrant like a cedar (Hos 14:6-9). The images could have come from Hosea himself, because they reflect themes of fertility and fruitfulness so popular in that prophet's thinking, but they were placed at the end by editors to give a final up-beat tone to the book. Micah ends with an expression of faith in the God whom tramples guilt, showing faithfulness to Jacob and grace to Abraham as of old (Mic 7:19-20). There remains a lingering doubt regarding whether the final chapters actually came from Micah himself, but there is no doubt about the inspired quality of these words as received by the leaders of God's people.

After the cacophony of terrifying judgment, each prophetic symphony had to end on a gentle harmonious note, at least that was the conviction of the pastoral personnel who put things in final order for synagogue assemblies. Was it false hope? Until the last act of the drama, we have only our faith as guide.

Sometimes the pastoral editors fashioned a call-story and placed it at the beginning to illustrate divine presence from the very inception of life, as in the case of young Jeremiah (Jer 1:4-19). At other times the call was placed in the very middle of things, as in the story of Amos (Am 7:12-17) or Isaiah (Is 6:1-9:6). In each case the strong negative judgments seemed so absolute and irreversible that a response of conversion on the part of the people was unlikely if not hopeless. The very location of the call in the book attempts to communicate the message.

A careful reader of Isaiah can observe the evidence of the editorial insertion, for woes abound before and after the call (Is 5:8. 11. 18. 20. 21. 22; 10:1. 5) and the threatening refrain is repeated, "For all this, his wrath is not turned back, and his hand is still out stretched" (5:25; 9:11. 16. 20; 10:4)! At some point it would seem that an editor, also under the inspiration of the Lord's revealing Spirit, inserted the previously independent text of 6:1-9:6 into the list of woes. What does it mean for the prophet to receive a call in the midst of such dire warnings? Is there any hope for personal satisfaction or for a sense of accomplishment?

In the book of Amos it almost seems as if hymns were added, celebrating the divine Name and its power over creation (Am 4:13; 5:8-9; 9:6). Perhaps some liturgist's care for synagogue worship triumphed again! Did a sensitive or delicate editor seek some relief from the drumming beat of death, or was it a theologian who knew that the judgments of Amos only represented a partial picture of larger reality? When does muting enhance the Word, making it more accurate? When does muting or recasting pervert it? This was a tough question which someone struggled with, especially in view of the Deuteronomic prohibition against any change (Dt 4:2).

Sometimes it was proverbs of one type or another which were interspersed throughout the text, inviting more deliberate attention. "The prudent person is silent at this time," says Amos, "for it is an evil time" (Am 5:13). A similar word to the wise forms the conclusion to the entire book of Hosea, as cited above, and gives pause to anyone who would ponder the full picture as applied to each successive generation (Hos 14:10). Does it fit our age? The editor almost forces the question. The book of Isaiah includes a summary of the way in which different grains are treated, and a final observation that this wisdom "comes from the Lord of hosts" (Is 28:29) just as prophetic oracles originate from God. Further reflection began to see revelation in a variety of human knowledges. Editors commissioned by the community to reshape the prophetic message into more usable form began to see the larger picture, as prophetic oracles, wise proverbs, melodic psalms and historical records were melded into a single commentary on God's dealings with the chosen people.

Entire collections of "Oracles against the Nations" were inserted into the text. It is probable that prophets traveled with the armies, encouraging them before each battle with promises of divine assistance. Priests may have been consulted regarding the wisdom of any given expedition and the will of the Lord in the matter (2 Chr 20:13-19). Gradually the names of traditional enemies were associated with heaped up opprobrium and promises of divine vengeance. The list of people denounced by Amos at Bethel may have been a very familiar one (Am 1:3-2:3).For the sake of completeness, extended oracles of judgment were inserted into each of the major prophetic works (Is 13-23; Jer 46-51; Ez 38-39). A complete picture of almost apocalyptic proportions was added to the book of Isaiah even later (Is 24-27), describing the final judgment and vindication of the city of Jerusalem. Editors who knew that God's salvation would be vindicated kept reciting the litany for courage and consolation. The books were taking shape, and it was faith which molded their contour.

It would seem that someone kept placing everything in a larger context.Even judgments which were proven correct by subsequent events, such as the devastating rejection of Israel, and then of Judah some hundred and forty years later, needed a larger horizon for correct understanding. In the last analysis as well as in the first, the God of the Hebrews was a saving God. That was the message, but first it had to become perfectly clear what depths of trouble could occur when human efforts were left to their own designs.

Biblical inspiration is unique, but the guidance of the Spirit hovers over every phase of the Word of God. First utterances and initial responses, later gathering and editing, then subsequent proclamation within the community of faith are all somehow included under the Spirit's care. So is the prayerful reflection on the text by modern readers!

Exile and New Beginnings

"Thus says the Lord, the God of Israel: 'Like these good figs, even so will I regard with favor Judah's exiles whom I sent away from this place into the land of the Chaldeans. I will look after them for their good, and bring them back to this land, to build them up, not to tear them down; to plant them, not to pluck them out!'" (Jer 24:5-6)

It may surprise even some of our informed readers that there were many exiles documented throughout the long history of Israel and Judah. Some Assyrian resettlement is suggested after the Syro-Ephramitic war in 733 B.C.E. (2 K 15:29; see 1 Chr 5:26). Another occurred after the destruction of Samaria in 722/21 B.C.E. (2 K 17:6; 18:11). Still another may have happened after Sennacherib's campaign against Hezekiah in Jerusalem (18:13-16) since archives of that infamous king of Assyria boasted of some 200,150 exiles from Judah. The figures were probably exaggerated propaganda, but something must have occurred at that time. Still other resettlements are mentioned in later books (Ez 4:2. 10). Prophets like Amos, Hosea, Isaiah and Micah were witnesses to some of these events.[1]

With the destruction of Nineveh in 613 B.C.E. the Babylonians came to power and after more than a century another series of exiles were written into the record. King Nebuchadnezzar captured Jerusalem in 597 B.C.E. and some

[1] See R. Sklba, "Until the Spirit from on High is Poured out on Us," *Catholic Biblical Quarterly* 46 (1984) 1-17.

10,000 of the nations leaders were sent off to the land of the
Euphrates (2 K 24:14-15). Ezekiel was probably in that group.
The great and terrible destruction of Jerusalem, and the
paragon for all exiles, occurred in July of 587/86 B.C.E. (25:7).
Given the serious theological nature and consequences of that
shattering event, we are surprised to learn of one record which
lists only 832 persons relocated after the fall of the city to
Babylon (Jer 52:29)! Finally there is a mysterious reference to
an additional 745 exiles in 582/1 B.C.E. (52:30). Although
Zephaniah, Nahum and Habakkuk may have witnessed the
decline of Assyria and rise of Babylon, only Jeremiah and
Ezekiel personally experienced the terrible trauma of this
brutal onslaught against Jerusalem.

From a theological as well as a political and human stand-
point, the fall and destruction of Jerusalem was a disaster of
enormous proportions. Yahweh had given his people a land
and a royal dynasty, a temple and a priesthood. Yahweh had
entered into covenant with them all and promised to bless and
protect them. Everything was destroyed and ripped away.
They were wrenched from their land, leaving only a few poor
villages to live in witness to the days of old and the sites once
sanctified by the Lord's name. Did the Lord's people exist as
such any more: Was Yahweh Himself the one who had been
badly beaten by the gods of Babylon? Was there any hope ever
again? These are questions which must be asked by every
person who feels herself faithful, but victimized or defeated in
a noble cause.

Watching all these forces converge for the show-down,
Habakkuk counseled patient waiting if the vision was mysteriously delayed (Hab 2:3). As Jeremiah watched the unraveling
of the royal court in Jerusalem, he was convinced that Israel
had in fact been more just than her southern sister Judah who

remained obstinate and unafraid through it all (Jer 3:8,11) Jeremiah used all the powers of persuasion at his command to encourage Judean soldiers to lay down their arms and surrender to the Babylonians. For this act of treason, he was jailed (37:1-21; 38:1-28). In this daring act he became the great patron of subsequent conscientious objectors. Those who witnessed all this turmoil could not conceive that the Lord could actually decree victory for Babylon. But so it was. When the walls had been destroyed and the dust settled, those leaders and royal officials still in place after the first capture of the city were once more marched off to exile in a foreign land.

Some few peasants remained to pray at the temple ruins and to cultivate whatever arable land remained. They felt slightly vindicated for they at least retained a bond to the land, even if as indentured serfs to a foreign nation. The leaders of the people and the royal family were in Babylon, visibly punished for their share in the sad affair. After the murder of Governor Gedaliah (40:13-41:18) some even fled to Egypt against the explicit advice of Jeremiah, dragging the prophet with them against his will (42:1-43:7). It was an evil time indeed. Amos was still correct (Am 5:13).

Of these three groups, namely those in Judah, in Babylon and in Egypt, which lived in continuity with the Chosen People? Were any of them heirs to the prophetic promises regarding the remnant? Would any enable the survival of God's People? Jeremiah pondered that dilemma. Once again he received a vision. He saw two baskets of figs, one excellent and early ripened, the other rotted and inedible. Jeremiah pronounced the exiles from the first capture of the city to be the chosen of the Lord represented by the basket of sweet ripe figs (Jer 24:1-7), and the inhabitants of Jerusalem who resisted Babylonian power to be the rotted group (vv. 8-10)!

To those exiles living in Babylon, Jeremiah sent word because they were being agitated by prophets of their own who insisted on a speedy return for all. It was a promise the prophet from Anatot could not support. Instead Jeremiah counseled them to "Build houses to dwell in; plant gardens and eat their fruits. Take wives and beget sons and daughters; find wives for your sons and give your daughters husbands, so that they may bear sons and daughters. There you must increase in number, not decrease. Promote the welfare (*shalom*) of the city to which I have exiled you; pray for it to the Lord, for upon its welfare (*shalom*) depends your own" (29:5-7)! Jeremiah envisioned long-term residence, promising at least seventy years (v. 10; see 25:11-12) and history vindicated his vision, not only in the length of time prior to release under Cyrus of Persia, but also in the spiritual strength and vitality of the Babylonian community, for the Talmud was to come from that renewed assembly.

While those who remained at the Temple site continued to gather for their lamentations (Lam 1:4-22), others dreamed of a restoration of Judah and all her glory. The fallen "hut of David" (Am 9:11) would someday be rebuilt, and the anointed branch of David's house restored to glory after the searing judgment (Is 4:2-6), with the smoking cloud of incense by day and the flaming fire of divine presence by night. Editors inserted into the text the promise of the restoration of both Judah and Israel, rejoicing that "In those days the house of Judah will join the house of Israel; together they will come from the land of the north to the land which I gave to your fathers as a heritage" (Jer 3:18).

Respect for the Sabbath was part of the ritual of the Hebrews from the beginning (Ex 20:8-11), but during the exile it took on even greater significance. This marked off the faithful exiles from their neighbors. The words of Jeremiah regarding the Sabbath were remembered and probably enlarged to give evidence of his support for the exiles near Babylon. Encouragement for the Sabbath was especially dear to the exiles and their editors (Jer 17:19-27). It was a time of new beginnings for proven institutions. Like modern Roman Catholics after the Second Vatican Council, they found themselves doing old things for better reasons and shedding the burdens no longer viewed as helpful to a life of faith.

Throughout the great exile the stories of God's dealings with the Hebrews were rehearsed. If their lives were not necessarily harsh because of enforced servitude as had been the case in Egypt centuries earlier, they were certainly in an alien land. The oppression which they experienced came from the strange gods which were so lavishly cultivated in the temples along the Euphrates. Their ancient songs no longer gave them joy (Ps 137:1-7). Ezekiel and his followers dreamed of a new land with a rebuilt Temple (Ez 40-48). The leaders of those in exile listened carefully, and heard repeatedly the sage advice appended to the final chapter of the book of Hosea: "Let the wise person understand these things!" (Hos 14:10).

They listened to the voice of an unknown prophet who promised new comfort and a new beginning (Is 40-55). With him or her, they sought to image the way in which the burning desert sand would be turned to pools of fresh water for the dusty travelers on their way back to Jerusalem (41:17-20). In the thinking of the exiles the Spirit of God became more intimately associated with the great events of their earlier liberation from Egypt (63:10-14). It was a time of great spiritual ferment and renewal. The treasures of their faith were once more spread out for the consolation and encouragement of the people.

Throughout it all, it became very clear that exile was not forever, no matter how much they may have deserved the tragic punishment and loss. The exiles also learned that the God of Israel would never allow a permanent "dead end" for his people. No situation, not even those deliberately caused by human stubbornness and sinfulness, was devoid of God's grace. Even modern war or divorce, even the deliberate destruction of beauty and goodness, remains somehow open to the grace of new beginnings for those who trust in Yahweh. God calls into being whatever he wills. He will be whatever he will be—always!

Those in Exile or others influenced by that experience read again the great prayer uttered by Solomon at the time of the dedication of the Temple. Having heard the threats and renewed promises of the pre-exilic prophets, they added a new paragraph to his prayer. It would remain a sign of hope forever.

Thus prayed Solomon: "When they sin against you (for there is no person who does not sin), and in your anger against them you deliver them to the enemy, so that their captors deport them to a hostile land, far or near, may they repent in the land of their captivity and be converted. If they entreat you in the land of their captors and say, 'We have sinned and done wrong; we have been wicked'; if with their whole heart and soul they turn back to you in the land of their enemies who took them captive, pray to you toward the land you gave their ancestors, the city you have chosen, and the Temple I have built in your honor, listen from your heavenly dwelling. Forgive your people their sins and all the offenses they have committed against you, and grant them mercy before their captors, so that these will be merciful to them. For they are your people and your inheritance, whom you brought out of Egypt, from the midst of an iron furnace" (1 K 8:45-51).

"So now I will deal with you in my own way, O Israel! And since I will deal thus with you, prepare to meet your God, O Israel!" (Am 4:12).

Bibliography

Further Reading

Following the wise counsel of Theresa of Avila, we note that healthy spirituality is based on intelligent understanding of the ways of God. For further nourishment and mental as well as spiritual stretching, consider the following resources:

General Works

J. Blenkinsopp, *A History of Prophecy in Israel* (Westminster, 1983).

W. Brueggemann, *The Prophetic Imagination* (Fortress, 1978).

M. Buber, *The Prophetic Faith* (Macmillan, 1949).

A. Heschel, *The Prophets* (Jewish Publication Society of America, 1962).

K. Koch, *The Prophets* (Fortress, 1982).

J. Lindblom, *Prophecy in Ancient Israel*(Fortress, 1962).

E. Maly, *Prophets of Salvation* (Herder and Herder, 1967).

C. Stuhlmueller, *The Prophets and the Word of God* (Fides, 1964).

G. von Rad, *The Message of the Prophets* (SCM Press, 1969).

H.W.Wolff, *Confrontations with Prophets* (Fortress, 1983).

Special Works on Samuel

H. Herzberg, *I and II Samuel: A Commentary;* Old Testament Library (Westminster, 1964).

P.K. McCarter, Jr., *I Samuel: A New Translation with Introduction, Notes and Commentary*; Anchor Bible 8 (Doubleday, 1980).

Special Works on Elijah

J. Gray, *I and II Kings: A Commentary*; Old Testament Library (Westminster, 1963).

B. Long, *I Kings with an Introduction to Historical Literature*; The Forms of Old Testament Literature 9 (W. Eerdmans, 1984).

Special Works on Amos

R. Coote, *Amos Among the Prophets: Composition and Theology* (Fortress, 1981).

A. Kapelrud, *Central Ideas in Amos* (Universitetsforlaget/Oslo, 1961).

J. Mays, *Amos: A Commentary*; Old Testament Library (Westminster, 1969).

J. Moytera, *The Day of the Lion: Prophet in an Era of Affluence* (Intervarsity Press, 1974).

J. Ward, *Amos and Isaiah* (Abingdon, 1969).

J. Watts, *Vision and Prophecy in Amos* (W. Eerdmans, 1958).

H.W. Wolff, *Amos the Prophet* (Fortress, 1973).

_____, *Joel and Amos: A Commentary on the Books of Joel and Amos*; Hermeneia (Fortress, 1977).

Special Works on Hosea

F. Anderson and D. Freedman, *Hosea: A New Translation with Introduction and Commentary*; Anchor Bible 24 (Doubleday, 1980).

W. Brueggemann, *Tradition for Crisis: A Study in Hosea* (John Knox Press, 1968).

J. Mays, *Hosea: A Commentary;* Old Testament Library (Westminster, 1969).

B. Vawter, *Amos, Hosea and Micah;* Old Testament Message 7 (Glazier, 1981).

J.Ward, *Hosea: A Theological Commentary* (Harper and Row, 1966).

H.W. Wolff, *Hosea: A Commentary on the Book of the Prophet Hosea;* Hermeneia (Fortress, 1974).

Special Works on Micah

D. Hillers, *Micah: A Commentary on the Book of the Prophet Micah;* Hermeneia (Fortress, 1984).

J. Mays, *Micah: A Commentary;* Old Testament Library (Westminster, 1976).

H.W. Wolff, *Micah the Prophet* (Fortress, 1978).

Special Works on First Isaiah
(Chapters 1-39)

S. Blank, *Prophetic Faith in Isaiah* (Wayne State University Press, 1967).

J. Jensen, *Isaiah 1-39;* Old Testament Message 8 (Glazier, 1984).

O. Kaiser, *Isaiah 1-12: A Commentary;* Old Testament Library (Westminster, 1972).

_____ , *Isaiah 13-39: A Commentary;* Old Testament Library (Westminster, 1974).

E. Leslie, *Isaiah* (Abingdon, 1963).

J.Schmitt, *Isaiah and His Interpreters* (Paulist, 1986).

Special Works on Zephaniah

A. Kapelrud, *The Message of the Prophet Zephaniah* (Universitetsfolget-/Oslo, 1975).

Special Works on Jeremiah

J. Berridge, *Prophet, People and the Word of God: An Explanation of Form and Content in the Proclamation of the Prophet Jeremiah* (EVZ Verlag/Zurich, 1970).

L. Boadt, *Jeremiah 1-25;* Old Testament Message 9 (Glazier, 1982).

J. Bright, *Jeremiah: Introduction, Translation and Notes;* Anchor Bible 21 (Doubleday, 1965).

R. Carroll, *From Chaos to Covenant* (Crossroads, 1981).

——————— , *Jeremiah: A Commentary;* Old Testament Library (Westminster, 1986).

W. Holloday, *Jeremiah: Spokesman Out of Time* (United Church Press, 1974).

——————— , *Jeremiah I: A Commentary on the Book of the Prophet Jeremiah,* Chapters 1-25; Hermeneia (Fortress, 1986).

E. Nicholson, *Preaching to the Exiles* (Blackwell, 1970).

T. Overholt, *The Threat of Falsehood;* Studies in Biblical Theology 16 (Allenson, 1970).

Special Studies on Habakkuk

D. Gowan, *The Triumph of Faith in Habakkuk* (John Knox Press, 1976).

Special Works on Ezekiel

W. Eichrodt, *Ezekiel: A Commentary;* Old Testament Library (Westminster, 1970).

W. Zimmerli, *Ezekiel I: A Commentary on the Book of the Prophet Ezekiel*, Chapters 1-24; Hermeneia (Fortress, 1979).

——————, *Ezekiel 2: A Commentary on the Book of the Prophet Ezekiel*, Chapters 25-48; Hermeneia (Fortress, 1983).

Specialized Studies

R. Bergren, *The Prophets and the Law* (Hebrew Union College, 1974).

J.Blenkinsopp, *Prophecy and Canon* (University of Notre Dame Press, 1977).

J. Bright, *Covenant and Promise* (Westminster, 1976).

R. Carroll, *When Prophecy Fails* (Crossroads, 1979).

R.E. Clements, *Prophecy and Covenant* (SCM Press, 1965).

——————, *Prophecy and Tradition* (John Knox Press, 1975).

J. Crenshaw, *Prophetic Conflict* (De Gruyter, 1971).

E.W. Davies, *Prophecy and Ethics* (University of Sheffield, 1981).

D. Hillers, *Treaty-Curses and the Old Testament Prophets* (Pontifical Biblical Institute, 1964).

A.R. Johnson, *The Cultic Prophet in Ancient Israel* (University of Wales Press, 1962).

W. McKane, *Prophets and Wisemen* (SCM Press, 1966).

E.R. Siegman, *The False Prophets of the Old Testament* (Catholic University of America, 1938).

R. Wilson, *Prophecy and Society in Ancient Israel* (Fortress, 1980).

Scripture Index

Subject Index